DATE			

FORM 125M

REAL ESTATE
MATHEMATICS
Simplified

REAL ESTATE MATHEMATICS
Simplified

SUSAN A. SHULMAN

ARCO PUBLISHING, INC.
NEW YORK

Published by Arco Publishing, Inc.
219 Park Avenue South, New York, N.Y. 10003

Library of Congress Cataloging in Publication Data

Shulman, Susan A.
  Real estate mathematics simplified

  1. Business mathematics—Real estate business.
2. Business mathematics—Real estate business—Problems, exercises, etc. I. Title.

HF5695.5.R37S55   513'.93   78-15542

ISBN 0-668-04713-5 (Paper Edition)

Printed in the United States of America

CONTENTS

ACKNOWLEDGMENTS

I would like to thank several people for their contributions to the successful completion of this book.

My thanks go to the directors of the Real Estate School of Central New Jersey, Edison, New Jersey, for providing me with the experience in teaching Real Estate Mathematics.

My appreciation goes to my mother, Shirley Krumholz, for her help in preparing the manuscript.

A special thanks to my husband, Marty, and my sons, Lawrence and Andrew for providing a loving atmosphere in which to write.

Susan A. Shulman

REAL ESTATE
MATHEMATICS
Simplified

HOW TO USE THIS BOOK

The Real Estate Licensing Examinations for salespeople and brokers require some knowledge and facility with mathematics. Questions will appear which can only be answered by applying your mathematical know-how.

This is a basic book designed to prepare you to successfully answer these questions. Everything you need to know about Real Estate Mathematics for passing your exam is in it. It assumes little or no familiarity with the subject. All new material is gradually introduced in the text to facilitate learning.

You will get maximum results from this book by applying the following procedure:

1. Take the Diagnostic Test. This will help you discover your areas of strength and weakness. The keyed answers following the Diagnostic Test will refer you to specific chapters in this text for review. Concentrate on those chapters in which you need the greatest help. The Diagnostic Test will also give you a general idea of the types of mathematical questions you can expect on the actual exam and will serve as a helpful guide in your methodical course of study.

2. Read Chapter 1. This chapter will provide you with all of the computational tools you will need for solving problems. For some this chapter will be a review, while for others who are weak in computation it will provide crucial information and practice. If you are planning to use a calculator don't forget to read Chapter 12.

3. Read Chapter 2. This chapter should be viewed as compulsory. In it, a key problem-solving technique is presented. This technique is used consistently throughout the text.

4. Read Chapters 3–10. Each chapter is organized so that you can follow these steps:
   a. Read the discussion which defines the type of problem.
   b. Study the sample basic problem.
   c. Become familiar with the variations on the basic problem.
   d. Study the solved practice problems.
   e. Do the unsolved practice problems whose solutions appear at the end of each chapter.

5. Read Chapter 11 only if you are taking the Broker's Exam. Follow the sequence described above for Chapters 3–10 in Chapter 11.

6. Take the appropriate Practice Exams at the end of the book. Remember that on the actual exam these types of questions will be distributed throughout the test.

This book can help you if you are willing to put in a little time and effort. Computation and problem-solving are often tedious but they **CAN** be mastered. Notice that the title of this book is not *Real Estate Mathematics Made Fun*, but rather *Real Estate Mathematics Simplified.*

DIAGNOSTIC TEST

Directions: Read the following problems and select the correct answer.
Indicate your choice by writing in the blank space provided.

1. Find $12\frac{1}{2}\%$ of 560
   (A) 348
   (B) 68.32
   (C) 70
   (D) 4480

2. 14 is ___% of 42?
   (A) 18%
   (B) 58%
   (C) 30%
   (D) $33\frac{1}{3}\%$

3. Change $\frac{3}{8}$ to a percent
   (A) $37\frac{1}{2}\%$
   (B) .375%
   (C) 2.6%
   (D) 26%

4. $2 \div .5 =$
   (A) .4
   (B) 40
   (C) .25
   (D) 4

5. $\frac{3}{4} \div 3 =$
   (A) $1\frac{1}{2}$
   (B) $2\frac{1}{4}$
   (C) $\frac{3}{7}$
   (D) $\frac{1}{4}$

6. Mr. Baker borrowed $15,000 from the bank. He pays $300 interest quarterly. At what rate of interest did he borrow the money?
   (A) 10%
   (B) 8%
   (C) $12\frac{1}{2}\%$
   (D) 2%

2

7. Mrs. Rothbart takes a bank loan for $2000 at an 8 percent annual interest rate. If the total interest she pays is $40 upon paying back the entire loan, for how long did she keep the money?
   (A) 3 months
   (B) 15 months
   (C) 1 year
   (D) 6 months

8. A salesman earns $8000 a year. He receives a salary of $350 per month plus commission at a rate of 6 percent on all sales if he sells more than $50,000 for the year. What were his total sales for the year?
   (A) $127,500
   (B) $133,333
   (C) $63,333
   (D) $113,333

9. A property's current appraisal is $40,000. If the original price, 5 years ago, was $32,000, find the average annual rate of appreciation.
   (A) 20%
   (B) 25%
   (C) 4%
   (D) 5%

10. A property is worth $5000. It appreciates 8 percent each year over the previous year's value. Find its value after 3 years.
    (A) $3800
    (B) $5120
    (C) $6300
    (D) $6200

11. Mrs. Ray invests $2000. After 2 years her investment is worth $2800. What is the average yearly rate of profit on her investment?
    (A) 75%
    (B) 70%
    (C) 20%
    (D) 40%

12. The closing on a home is March 15. If the seller pre-paid taxes of $900 on the first of the year, which of the following was true at closing?
    (A) The buyer owed the seller $187.50.
    (B) The seller owed the buyer $187.50.
    (C) The buyer owed the seller $712.50.
    (D) The seller owed the buyer $712.50.

13. What is the difference in taxes on a $40,000 home between a tax rate of $3.25/$100 and $.43/$10, if the home is assessed at 75 percent of its value?
    (A) $975
    (B) $315
    (C) $500
    (D) $846

14. What fraction of the diagram below is shaded?

    (A) $\frac{8}{25}$
    (B) $\frac{4}{25}$
    (C) $\frac{25}{4}$
    (D) $\frac{1}{3}$

15. A $1\frac{1}{2}$ acre lot is purchased at $2000. It is divided into 6 lots, each selling for $500. What is the net profit gained on the sale?

    (A) $2500
    (B) $1000
    (C) $0
    (D) $500

16. Find 120% of $6\frac{1}{2}\%$.

    (A) 75%
    (B) .75%
    (C) $7\frac{1}{2}\%$
    (D) 19%

17. Convert 216 cubic feet to cubic yards.

    (A) 12 cubic yards
    (B) 24 cubic yards
    (C) 5832 cubic yards
    (D) 8 cubic yards

18. On a $50,000 loan taken at a 9 percent interest rate for 25 years, find the monthly payments if each month's installment is $8.50 per $1000.

    (A) $153
    (B) $425
    (C) $500
    (D) $360

ANSWER KEY

The chapter in parentheses following each correct answer refers to the chapter in this text where material concerning the question is discussed.

1.	C (Chapter 1)	10.	C (Chapter 6)
2.	D (Chapter 1)	11.	C (Chapter 5)
3.	A (Chapter 1)	12.	C (Chapter 9)
4.	D (Chapter 1)	13.	B (Chapter 8)
5.	D (Chapter 1)	14.	B (Chapter 10)
6.	B (Chapter 3)	15.	B (Chapter 7)
7.	A (Chapter 3)	16.	C (Chapter 1)
8.	D (Chapter 4)	17.	D (Chapter 10)
9.	D (Chapter 6)	18.	B (Chapter 3)

1

BASIC COMPUTATIONAL SKILLS

This chapter deals with a review of the basic skills which should be mastered for the Real Estate Licensing Exams. Even with the use of a calculator during the exam, it is risky to rely solely on a machine. The basic skills should be mastered if only to check that the calculator has not gone berserk. If you feel competent in working with percents and decimals you should proceed to Chapter 2.

PERCENTS AND DECIMALS

The first fact to learn is that percents and decimals are simply numbers written in a form different from that which we are usually accustomed.

The word "percent" means "per hundred" or "out of one hundred." Therefore, 100 percent means 100 out of 100; 50 percent means 50 out of 100; 17 percent means 17 out of 100.

What does 25% mean? _____ out of _____
What does 62% mean? _____ out of _____

We cannot compute with percents. We must be able to change percents to decimal form in order to compute. Let us see how this is done.

One place after the decimal point is the tenths place. Therefore, .6 means 6 tenths or 6 out of 10. Two places after the decimal point is the hundredths place. Therefore, .25 means 25 hundredths or 25 out of 100. Notice we just used the expression 25 out of 100 for 25 percent.

Therefore,

$$25\% = 25 \text{ out of } 100 = .25$$
$$\text{or}$$
$$25\% = .25$$

Obviously, we are not going to go through this procedure each time we want to change percents to decimals. All we are looking for is a quick and easy rule. The rule is as follows:

TO CHANGE A PERCENT TO A DECIMAL MOVE THE DECIMAL POINT TWO PLACES TO THE LEFT.

Change these percents to decimals.

16% = _____
20% = _____
45% = _____
32% = _____

When dealing with real estate problems we often work with percents that are less than 10 percent, such as 4 percent, 5 percent, etc. How can we change these to decimals? Just by following the same basic rule, we must move the decimal point two places to the left. (Whenever the decimal point is not shown, it is assumed to be at the end of the number.) With 4% or 4.%, if we try to move the decimal point two places to the left while dropping the % sign, we find that we don't have two places to go to the left. It would not be "illegal" to write 4.% as 04.%. The extra zero in front of the 4 is put there just for our convenience. It does not change the value of the original number.

So 4% = 4.% = 04.%. Moving the decimal point two places to the left we see that 4% = .04. (Remember to drop the % sign as soon as the decimal point is moved to the proper place.)

$$5\% = .05$$
$$6\% = \underline{\hspace{2cm}}$$
$$8\% = \underline{\hspace{2cm}}$$
$$9\% = \underline{\hspace{2cm}}$$

Sometimes we are working with numbers that are greater than 100 percent, such as 125 percent (125% = 125.%). Again, just following our rule we move the decimal point two places to the left.

$$125\% = 125.\% = 1.25$$

Try these:

$$165\% = \underline{\hspace{2cm}}$$
$$122\% = \underline{\hspace{2cm}}$$
$$200\% = \underline{\hspace{2cm}}$$
$$183\% = \underline{\hspace{2cm}}$$

Sometimes we are required to work with half-percents, such as $25\frac{1}{2}$ percent. We would like to change this to decimal form. It is the fraction that is getting in our way. There is one easy way to get around half-percents. We know that $\frac{1}{2} = \frac{5}{10}$. Therefore, $25\frac{1}{2}$ percent can be written as 25.5 percent (since $\frac{5}{10} = .5$). Now once again, just following the easy rule, move the decimal point two places to the left to give us 25.5% = .255.

Change the following percents to decimals:

$$35\frac{1}{2}\% = \underline{\hspace{2cm}}$$
$$125\frac{1}{2}\% = \underline{\hspace{2cm}}$$
$$5\frac{1}{2}\% = \underline{\hspace{2cm}}$$

Suppose we were given the fraction $12\frac{1}{4}$ percent with which to compute. Again, it is the fraction that is getting in our way. We would like to be able to change this fraction to decimal form. It was easy when we were changing $\frac{1}{2}$ percent; other fractions require another step. The fraction line says *divide*. The fraction $\frac{1}{4}$ means 1 divided by 4 or

$$4\overline{\smash{)}\,1.00}^{\,.25}$$

Therefore $12\frac{1}{4}\% = 12.25\% = .1225$.

If you are using a calculator, it is easy to change any fraction to a decimal by dividing the numerator (top number) by the denominator (bottom number). To change $\frac{1}{4}$ to a decimal by using the calculator, simply press 1, press $\div$, press 4, and press =. The .25 will appear in the display.

It is very important that you do not get very analytical, as human nature would have it, and question, "Why should $12\frac{1}{4}$ percent equal .1225"? **JUST USE THE RULES.** Save all mathematical theory for after the exam.

It makes sense that if we change a percent to a decimal by moving the decimal point two places to the left, to change a decimal to a percent we must move the decimal two places to the right and add a percent sign.

For example:

$$.85 = 85\%$$
$$.06 = \ 6\%$$
$$.035 = 3.5\% \text{ or } 3\frac{5}{10}\% \text{ or } 3\frac{1}{2}\%$$

Change the following to a percent:

$$.63 \ = \text{_____}$$
$$.07 \ = \text{_____}$$
$$1.35 \ = \text{_____}$$
$$.455 = \text{_____}$$

Do the following exercises to review percents and decimals:

1. 82% means _____ out of _____.
2. 63% means _____ out of _____.
3. Change 45% to a decimal. _____
4. Change 3% to a decimal. _____
5. Change 130% to a decimal. _____
6. Change .57 to a percent. _____
7. Change .02 to a percent. _____
8. Change $6\frac{1}{5}\%$ to a decimal. _____
9. .065 = _____%
10. $\dfrac{42}{100}$ = _____%

Basic Operations with Decimals

Once we have changed percents to decimals we are often required to add, subtract, multiply, and divide with decimals to arrive at our final answer.

Addition with Decimals

To add decimals it is easiest to write one number under another, making sure to line up all of the decimal points. Remember that if any number appears to have no decimal point it is assumed to be at the end of the number. For example, 16 = 16.

To add 1.63 + .035 + 19 + 162, we write:

$$
\begin{array}{r}
1.63 \\
.035 \\
19. \\
\underline{162. } \\
\end{array}
$$

If you feel more comfortable having a more uniform looking problem, you can use zeros to fill empty spaces.

$$
\begin{array}{r}
1.630 \\
.035 \\
19.000 \\
\underline{162.000} \\
182.665
\end{array}
$$

Subtraction with Decimals

To subtract decimals, again line up decimal points:

$$
\begin{array}{r}
1.83 \\
\underline{-.06} \\
1.77
\end{array}
$$

Zeros are compulsory as fillers in subtraction. For example:

$$
\begin{array}{r}
18.6 \\
\underline{-3.42}
\end{array}
$$

We must add a zero after the 6 so that we can do the problem.

$$
\begin{array}{r}
18.60 \\
\underline{-3.42} \\
15.18
\end{array}
$$

Multiplication with Decimals

To multiply decimals, apply the following procedure:

1. Change all percents to decimals.
2. Multiply both numbers, disregarding the decimal points.
3. Total the number of decimal places to the right of the decimal point in both numbers.
4. Make sure this total number of decimal places after the decimal points is the same as the number of decimal places after the decimal point in the answer.

For example: 22% × 1200

1. 22% = .22
2. 22 × 1200 = 26400
3. There are two decimal places after the decimal in .22 and zero decimal places after the decimal in 1200, for a total of two all together.
4. The answer is 264.00 or 264.

Division with Decimals

Division that involves decimals requires that there are no decimals in the divisor (that is, the number on the outside of the division sign). Therefore, if we wanted to divide 10.25 by 2.5, we would first have to eliminate the decimal in the divisor, 2.5. It would be most convenient to move the decimal point one place to the right so that we could divide by 25. If we move the decimal point in the divisor, we are then obligated to do the same to the number we are dividing (that is, the number on the inside of the division sign). Therefore, we would also have to move the decimal point in 10.25 one place to the right. We would then have 102.5. While this procedure was necessary in order to eliminate the decimal in the divisor, decimals appearing in the number inside the division sign do not have to be eliminated. We now have

$$2.5 \overline{\smash{)}10.25}$$

$$25 \overline{\smash{)}102.5}$$

The decimal point in the answer is placed right above the decimal point in the dividend (the number inside the division sign). Once the decimal points are in the correct positions we divide as if they were not there at all. In the preceding problem the answer would be 4.1. In division of decimals, the correct procedures are as follows:

1.   Move the decimal point in the number outside the division sign until it is all the way to the right.
2.   Move the decimal point of the number inside the same number of places to the right.
3.   Put the decimal in the answer space right above where it is in the inside number.
4.   Divide as usual.

$$25 \overline{\smash{)}\overset{4.1}{102.5}}$$

Divide the following:

(1) $8.1 \overline{\smash{)}1.62}$

(2) $1.5 \overline{\smash{)}30}$ (Hint: 30 = 30.)

FRACTIONS

Fractions can be dealt with very easily by changing them to decimals. Remember, the fraction line says "divide." Therefore, to change a fraction to a decimal, we divide the numerator by the denominator. To change $\frac{1}{5}$ to a decimal, we do the following:

$$5 \overline{\smash{)}1} \ =$$

$$5 \overline{\smash{)}1.00} \ =$$

$$5 \overline{\smash{)}\overset{.20}{1.00}}$$

Change the following fractions to decimals:

$$\frac{1}{8} = \underline{\hspace{2cm}}$$

$$\frac{3}{4} = \underline{\hspace{2cm}}$$

$$\frac{1}{12} = \underline{\hspace{2cm}}$$

Fractions Used to Compare Numbers

We can use a fraction to help us to compare two numbers. Suppose we want to compare the area of a building to the area of the lot on which it is built. The area of a building is 1500 square ft., compared to the area of the lot which is 15,000 square ft. The fraction 1500/15,000 expresses the relationship. The number that we are comparing "to" always goes in the denominator (bottom of the fraction). In the preceding example we are comparing the area of a building to the area of a lot. Therefore, the area of the lot goes in the denominator. If we also wanted to know what percent the area of the building was in relation to the area of the lot, we would first change the fraction 1500/15,000 to a decimal and then to a percent.

$$1500/15,000 = 15,000 \overline{) 1500.00}^{.10} = .10 = 10\%$$

In changing fractions to decimals it is best to carry the answer out to two places after the decimal point. If our answer does not work out evenly to two places after the decimal, we can round our answer off using the following rule:

If the number in the third place after the decimal is less than 5 we drop it; if the number in the third place after the decimal is 5 or more we add one to the number in the second place. For example:

.333 would be rounded off to .33
.647 would be rounded off to .65
.855 would be rounded off to .86

Exercises

1. Change $\frac{4}{5}$ to a decimal. _____
2. Change $\frac{1}{8}$ to a decimal. _____
3. Change $\frac{5}{12}$ to a decimal; to a % _____ ; _____
4. $\frac{3}{10}$ = _____ %
5. $\frac{7}{15}$ = _____ %
6. $\frac{1}{3}$ = _____ %
7. $\frac{2}{7}$ = _____ %

SOLUTIONS TO EXERCISES

Page 5

25 out of 100
62 out of 100

Page 5

.16
.20
.45
.32

Page 6

.06
.08
.09
1.65
1.22
2.00
1.83
.355
1.255
.055

Page 7

63%
7%
135%
$45\frac{1}{2}$%

Page 7

1. 82 out of 100
2. 63 out of 100
3. .45
4. .03
5. 1.30
6. 57%
7. 2%
8. .062
9. $6\frac{1}{2}$%
10. 42%

Page 9

.125
.75
.08

Page 10

1. .80
2. .125
3. .42 = 42%
4. 30%
5. .47 = 47%
6. $33\frac{1}{3}$%
7. .29 = 29%

2

A SHORTCUT METHOD TO SOLVING FORMULAS

Throughout this book many formulas will be presented. Mathematically, a formula is an equation which can help us to find things that we don't know, using the information that we do know. Algebra is a means of solving formulas. However, many of those preparing for the Real Estate Exams have never taken algebra or have forgotten it due to lack of use. This chapter is dedicated to a shortcut method that has been around for awhile to help the problem solver solve problems without the use of algebra. Not all formulas can be solved with this method. We will use it for formulas which have a specific form; that is, whenever we have two numbers multiplied to yield a result. As many formulas as possible will be put into this form throughout the book. To explain this shortcut method, the formula for finding the area of a rectangle will be used. It does fit the qualifications of having two numbers multiplied to yield a third. This formula is

Length X Width = Area

We start by using a triangle diagram as a visual aid, having nothing to do with the triangle as a geometric figure. We place the formula into the triangle in a specific way. Look at the diagram below.

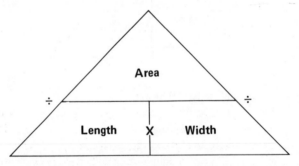

We always place the two variables in the formula which are being multiplied in the bottom spaces of the triangle and the one variable that they are equal to on the top of the triangle, as shown above. The horizontal line of the triangle says "divide" and the vertical line of the triangle says "multiply." When we read the triangle from top to bottom we divide, and when we read the triangle from left to right we multiply.

Suppose we knew that the area of a rectangle was 30 square ft., and the length was 10 ft. We were asked to find the width. We would set up the triangle as follows

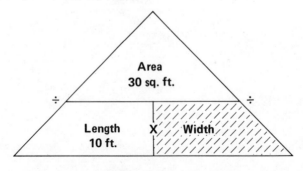

We shade out the one unknown in the problem as our first step. To find the width, we just read the triangle from top to bottom. Therefore, the width is equal to 30 divided by 10 or 3 ft.

Suppose we were told that the area = 30 square ft. and the width = 3 ft. We were asked to find the length of the rectangle. We would set up the triangle as follows

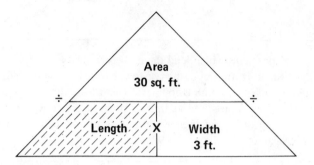

The Length would equal 30 divided by 3 or 10 ft.

Suppose we were told that the length = 10 ft. and the width = 3 ft. We were asked to find the area. We would set up the triangle as follows

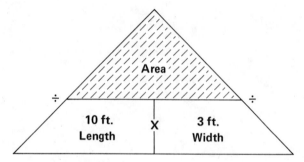

The Area would equal 10 X 3 = 30 square ft.

Notice in setting up the triangle that the two that are being multiplied always occupy the bottom spaces, and the one they are equal to, after being multiplied, goes on top. We must know two out of three facts to be able to solve for the third unknown fact. We simply shade out the one unknown and then read the triangle from top to bottom or from left to right to solve for the unknown.

If one forgets what goes where, just think of a simple multiplication problem such as 2 X 5 = 10 to refresh your memory. Such an equation would go into the triangle as follows

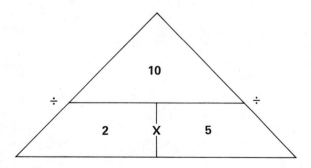

We can check that this is right, since we know 10 ÷ 2 = 5; 10 ÷ 5 = 2; and 2 X 5 = 10. If we misplaced these numbers we would have found our errors quickly.

Remember, not every problem can make use of the triangle method. However, when we do have two numbers multiplied to yield a third, the method can be very useful. This method will be used consistently throughout the book, whenever appropriate.

There are four types of word problems which lend themselves to similar solutions. In each type we are dealing with a base sum of money which is multiplied by a percent (rate) to yield a portion of that original sum. These four types of problems are interest, commission, profit and loss. In all four we can utilize the triangle method. All four can be varied and even disguised at times. However, once we get attuned to the terminology which helps us to spot and categorize these and their variations, it becomes easy to arrive at our solution. Each of these types will be dealt with separately in the next few chapters.

3
INTEREST

In the basic interest problem we have the base sum, being the principal or mortgage or loan, multiplied by a rate of interest, to give us the yearly interest. In short, we have the following formula:

Principal X Rate of Interest = Interest (yearly)

or

P X R = I (yearly)

We are able to set up the triangle to help work out the solutions for our basic problem. It will look like this:

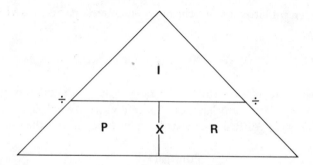

Notice that since the P and R are multiplied to yield the Interest they will occupy the bottom spaces in the triangle. The interest being by itself in the equation goes on top.

Note: No matter what information has been supplied in the problem, the P and the R always go on the bottom and the I goes on top.

Sample Basic Interest Problem

A yearly interest payment of $840 is made on a loan at a rate of 7 percent. What was the principal?

Solution

The key words in this problem are interest payment, rate of 7 percent and principal. These should start us to think about interest problems.

Principal = P = ?
Rate of Interest = R = 7% = .07
Interest = I = $840

We know that P X R = I. P and R will occupy the bottom the triangle and the I will go on the top.

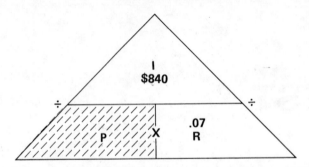

To find P we shade out the P box and just read the triangle from top to bottom. Therefore, P = 840 ÷ .07 = $12,000.

This basic interest problem can be varied very simply. Instead of being given the yearly interest we are sometimes given the interest payment for only part of a year as shown in the following variation.

VARIATION 1

A loan is made at an 8 percent interest rate. The quarterly interest payment is $150. Find the principal.

Solution

It would be human nature to plunge right in and assume that I, the interest, is $150. **WRONG!** In the formula P × R = I, the I refers to the *yearly* interest. Therefore, we are obligated to multiply quarterly interest of $150 by 4 to give us $600 as the yearly interest. We can now proceed with the basic interest problem again.

Principal = P = ?
Rate of Interest = R = 8% = .08
Interest = I = $600.

Using the triangle

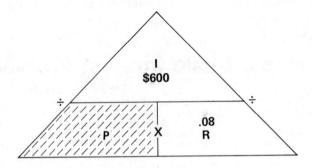

Principal = $600 ÷ .08 = $7500.

VARIATION 2

Mr. Smith borrowed $5200 from the bank for a new business at a 7 percent interest rate. If he repaid principal and interest in one payment at the end of 6 months, how much was the total amount he paid to the bank at the end of that 6 month period?

Solution

We can begin by using the basic formula, P X R = I, keeping in mind that we will first derive the yearly interest payment. Furthermore, since Mr. Smith kept the money for only 6 months, he must pay only one-half of the yearly interest. Finally, he will be paying back the sum of the loan and this half year's interest in one lump sum.

Principal = P = $5200
Rate of Interest = R = 7% = .07
Interest = I = ?

Using the triangle

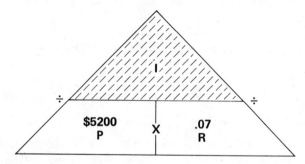

Interest (yearly = $5200) X .07 = $364.
One-half Year's Interest = $364 ÷ 2 = $182.

Finally, since Mr. Smith paid back the principal and interest combined after 6 months, he paid a total of $5200 + $182 = $5382.

VARIATION 3

In one popular type of interest problem too much information is given. We must be careful to use only what is actually needed. When working any mathematics problem, it is tempting to use all given numbers. After all, why would one be given a number if it wasn't needed? This is not always appropriate thinking. Consider the following:

SELLING PRICE	AMOUNT OF LOAN	TERMS OF LOAN	MONTHLY PAYMENT
From $40,000–$50,000	80%	9% – 30 yrs.	$9/$1000

Based on the table above, how much more are payments per month on a $48,000 home than on a $44,000 home?

Solution

The loan issued is only 80 percent of the selling price. Therefore, a loan on a $48,000 home will be 80 percent of $48,000 or .80 X $48,000 or $38,400. The loan on a $44,000 home will be 80 percent of $44,000 or 80 percent X $44,000 or .80 X $44,000 or $35,200.

The key to this problem is to realize that the terms of the loan, 9% – 30 years, is unnecessary information. The reason this is unnecessary is that we are simply being told that the payments per month are $9 per $1000. All we have to do is to find out how many 1000-dollar groups there are in the $38,400 and in $35,200 and then multiply each one of these by $9.

$$\$38,400 \div \$1000 = 38.4*$$
$$38.4 \times \$9 = \$345.60$$

$$\$35,200 \div \$1000 = 35.2*$$
$$35.2 \times \$9 = \$316.80$$

We have a difference in montly payments on a $48,000 home and a $44,000 home of $345.60 - $316.80 = $28.80.

*Moving a decimal three places to the left is the same as dividing by 1000.

VARIATION 4

A man pays $85 per month toward principal and interest on a $10,000 loan which was borrowed at 6 percent interest. How much of the principal remains after the first monthly payment?

Solution

There are two parts to this problem. For the first part, a circle diagram is used just as a visual aid. The circle will represent the monthly payment of $85 going toward interest and reducing the original loan.

This circle is worth $85.

If we knew exactly how much money went toward paying interest for the first month, it would be easy to figure out how much went toward reducing the principal. For example, if we knew that $60 went toward interest, then $25 would be left for reducing principal. If $75 went toward interest, then $10 would be left for reducing principal. Although we were not told right off how much the first month's interest is, we are given enough information to find this out. For this, we will again use the basic formula and the triangle.

$$P \times R = I$$
Principal = P = $10,000
Rate of Interest = R = 6% = .06
Interest = I = ?

Using the triangle

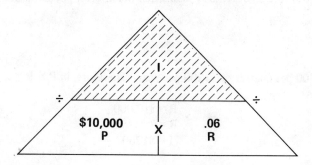

I = $10,000 × .06 = $600.

Therefore, if the yearly interest = $600, then the first montly interest payment is $600 ÷ 12 = $50. Using the circle, if interest = $50, then $85 – $50 or $35 must go toward reducing principal.

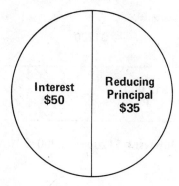

Furthermore, after the first month $10,000 – $35 or $9965 is left as the principal.

Interest Problems with Solutions

1. If the yearly interest on a $5000 loan is $400, what is the yearly rate of interest?

Solution

Using the basic formula P × R = I

$$P = \$5000$$
$$R = ?$$
$$I = \$400$$

Using the triangle

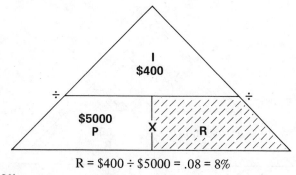

R = $400 ÷ $5000 = .08 = 8%

The Rate of Interest is 8%.

2.   What is the annual interest rate on a $12,000 loan when the interest payments are $300 per quarter?

Solution

Interest payments = $300 per quarter or $1200 per year. Therefore, in P × R = I,

P = $12,000
R = ?
I = $1200

Using the triangle

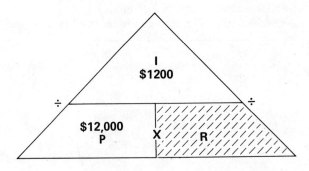

Rate of Interest = $1200 ÷ 12,000 = .10 = 10%

The Annual Interest Rate is 10%.

3.   Mrs. Barker borrowed $3500 from the bank at an interest of 9 percent on the original amount per year. At the end of 18 months, she repaid the loan and interest in one payment. How much was the total amount she paid to the bank?

Solution

P × R = I
P = $3500
R = 9% = .09
I = ?

Using the triangle

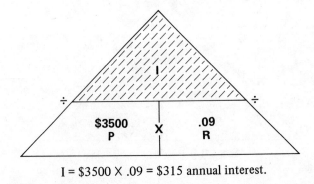

I = $3500 × .09 = $315 annual interest.

Since Mrs. Barker kept the money for 18 months or $1\frac{1}{2}$ years, the interest she owed was $315 × 1.5 = 472.50. The loan of $3500 added to the $472.50 interest due yields one payment of $3972.50 at the end of 18 months.

She repaid $3972.50.

4. Consider the following:

SELLING PRICE	AMOUNT OF LOAN	TERMS OF LOAN	MONTHLY PAYMENT
From $35,000–$45,000	75%	$8\frac{3}{4}$% – 30 years	$8/$1000

Based on the above chart, how much more are payments per month on a $36,000 home than on a $41,000 home?

Solution

$$\$36,000 \text{ home} - \text{Loan} = 75\% \text{ of } \$36,000 = .75 × \$36,000 = \$27,000$$

Monthly Payments = $8/$1000. To find how many thousands there are in $27,000 divide $27,000 by 1000. There are 27 thousands in $27,000. 27 × $8 = $216 per month for the $36,000 home.

$$\$41,000 \text{ home} - \text{Loan} = 75\% \text{ of } \$41,000 = .75 × \$41,000 = \$30,750.$$

Monthly Payments = $8/$1000. To find how many thousands there are in $30,750, divide $30,750 by 1000. There are 30.75 thousands in $30,750. 30.75 × $8 = $246 per month for the $41,000 home. The difference between the monthly payments is $246 – $216 = $30 per month.

She would pay $30 per month more.

5. A man pays $100 per month which goes toward interest due and reducing the $12,000 loan which was borrowed at an interest rate of 8 percent. How much principal remains after the first monthly payment?

Solution

This circle is worth $100

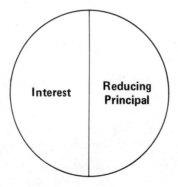

To find the first month's interest payment we use $P \times R = I$.

$$P = \$12,000$$
$$R = 8\% = .08$$
$$I = ?$$

(First we will find the yearly interest and then we will proceed to find the monthly interest.)

Using the triangle

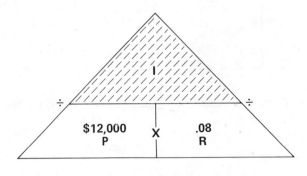

$$I = \$12,000 \times .08 = \$960$$

Interest Per Month = $\$960 \div 12 = \$80$. Putting this into a circle diagram

This circle is worth $100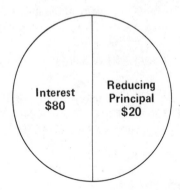

We know that $100 - $80 or $20 goes toward reducing principal. The amount of principal remaining after one month is $12,000 - $20 = $11,980.

$11,980 is due.

Practice Interest Problems

1. Mr. Dainoff borrowed $3000, on which he agreed to pay 8 percent interest annually. If he paid a total of $100 interest, for how long did he keep the money?

2. The mortgage balance is $6000, the monthly payments are $90 to principal, interest, tax, and insurance. Tax and insurance cost $408 annually. What is the principal amount owed after the first monthly payment has been applied if the annual interest rate is 8 percent?

3. What is the annual interest rate on a $9000 loan when the payments are $180 per quarter on the loan?

4. If the yearly interest payment is $960 on a 7 percent interest loan, what is the principal?

5. The loan on a house is 80 percent of the selling price. If the house sells for $40,000 and the monthly payment is $8.50 per $1000, what is the yearly loan payment?

6. In 1978 a bank's interest rate is 120 percent of its 1977 rate of $5\frac{1}{2}$ percent. Find the interest rate for 1978.

Solutions

1. First we find the yearly interest payment using $P \times R = I$.

$$P = \$3000$$
$$R = 8\% = .08$$
$$I = ?$$

Using the triangle

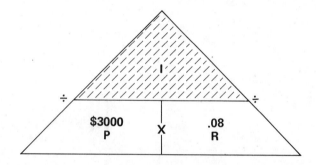

Yearly Interest = $3000 × .08 = $240. We know $240 ÷ 12 or $20 is one month's interest.

$$\$100 \div 20 = 5$$

Mr. Dainoff kept the money for 5 months.

2.

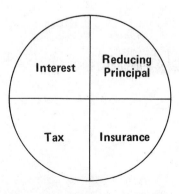

If tax and insurance cost $408 annually, they must cost 408 ÷ 12 = $34 per month.

So

Once we find the monthly interest payment, it will be easy to determine the amount that is left to be applied to principal. We determine the yearly interest first by using $P \times R = I$.

$$P = \$6000$$
$$R = 8\% = .08$$
$$I = ?$$

Using the triangle

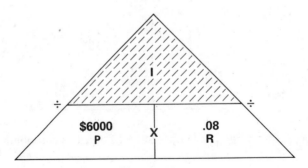

we find $I = \$6000 \times .08 = \$480$ per year or $40 per month. Now we have the following diagram

The circle is worth
$90 per month

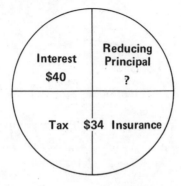

Since tax, insurance, and interest add up to $74 per month and the monthly payment is $90 per month, then $90 – $74 = $16 must go toward principal. This leaves $6000 – $16 = $5984 principal remaining after the first month.

3. Interest payments = $180 per quarter or $720 per year. In P × R = I

$$P = \$9000$$
$$R = ?$$
$$I = \$720$$

Using the triangle method

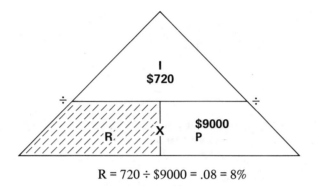

$$R = 720 \div \$9000 = .08 = 8\%$$

The Interest Rate is 8%.

4. Using P × R = I

$$P = ?$$
$$R = 7\% = .07$$
$$I = \$960$$

Using the triangle method

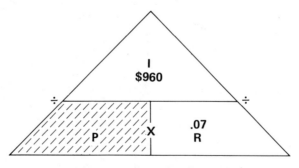

$$\text{Principal} = \$960 \div .07 = \$13,714.29$$

The Principal is $13,714.29.

5. Loan = 80 percent of $40,000 or .80 × $40,000 = $32,000. The monthly payment is $8.50 per thousand. We divide $32,000 by 1000 to find that there are 32 thousands in $32,000.

$$\$32 \times \$8.50 = \$272 \quad \text{(monthly payment)}$$
$$\$272 \times 12 = \$3264 \text{ (yearly payment)}$$

The Yearly loan payment is $3264.

6.   120% of $5\frac{1}{2}\%$ =
      120% $\times$ $5\frac{1}{2}\%$ =
      1.20 $\times$ .055 =
      .066 = 6.6%
      The Interest Rate is 6.6%.

4

COMMISSION

Selling Price X Rate of Commission is the formula used in the basic commission problem. The triangle method can be used again as follows

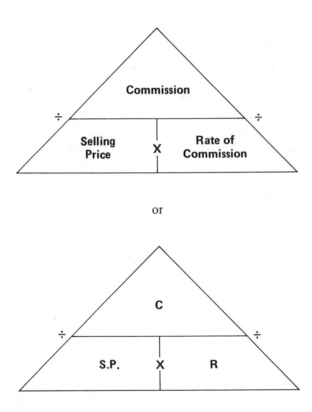

or

Sample Basic Commission Problem

A broker was paid an 8 percent commission on the sale of a home. He earned $4320 commission. What was the selling price?

Selling Price = ?
Rate of Commission = 8% = .08
Commission = $4320

Using the triangle method

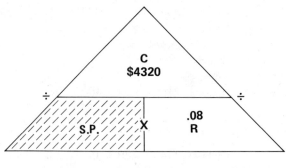

Selling Price = $4320 ÷ .08 = $54,000

VARIATION 1

A common variation of commission problems deals with a broker or a salesperson earning commission at two different rates. For example:

A broker earns 5 percent commission on the first $10,000 of a sale and 2 percent commission on anything sold over that amount. How much commission did he earn if he sold a $22,000 home?

Solution

Since we are working with two different rates of commission, it would be appropriate if we used two different triangles, as follows

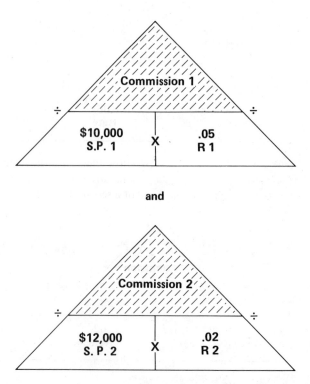

and

We can let $10,000 be Selling Price 1 (that is, the portion of the sale which earns commission at a rate of 5 percent). The balance of the selling price would be $22,000 - $10,000 = $12,000 (that is, the portion of the sale which earns commission at a 2 percent rate).

In Triangle 1 we can find Commission 1 by multiplying

$$\text{Commission } 1 = \$10,000 \times .05 = \$500$$

In Triangle 2 we can find Commission 2 by multiplying

$$\text{Commission } 2 = \$12,000 \times .02 = \$240$$

The Total Commission would be $500 + $240 = $740.

VARIATION 2

The above problem can be further varied in the following way:

A broker earns a fee of 6 percent commission on the first $12,000 of the sale and 3 percent of anything over that amount. The broker's fee on the sale was $900. What was the sale price?

Solution

We can again use two triangles since we are working with two rates of commission. We must plunge right into this problem to see if the broker sold at least the initial $12,000 at a 6 percent rate of commission. Using the triangle method

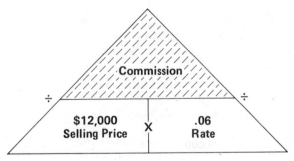

Commission would equal $12,000 × .06 or $720. We now know that the broker sold more than $12,000, since he earned $900 commission. This is $180 more than he would have made had he sold only $12,000 or less. To find out how much more than $12,000 he sold, we make use of a second triangle.

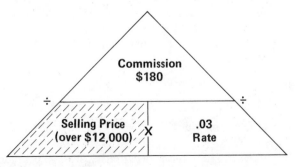

The Selling Price over $12,000 = $180 ÷ .03 = $6000.

Therefore, the first part of the sales price was $12,000 and the second part of the selling price was $6000, for a total sales price of $18,000.

VARIATION 3

Another type of commission problem involves the word **ratio**. This sounds more difficult than it really is.

A broker and salesperson share commission on a sale in the ratio of 5 to 3 (this can also be written as 5:3), respectively, on a sale of $40,000 with a 5 percent commission rate. How much more than the salesperson does the broker earn?

Solution

Before getting into ratio and deciding who gets what, it would be appropriate to first find the actual commission that is being divided. For this we use the triangle method.

The Commission to be Divided = $40,000 × .05 = $2000. Now we want to see where the word ratio comes in. We can think of ratio as parts. In this problem, the broker gets 5 parts compared to the salesperson's 3 parts, for a total of 8 parts. If we divide the $2000 commission by 8, we will see how much 1 part is worth. Then we simply assign 5 of these parts to the broker and 3 of these parts to the salesperson.

$$\$2000 \div 8 = \$250$$
$$1 \text{ part} = \$250$$
$$5 \text{ parts} = \$250 \times 5 = \$1250$$
$$3 \text{ parts} = \$250 \times 3 = \$750$$

The broker gets 5 parts or $1250; the salesperson gets 3 parts or $750. The broker earns $500 more than the salesperson.

> **NOTE:** If three people A, B, and C shared commission in the ratio of 4:3:2, we would first find the commission to be divided and divide it by 4 + 3 + 2, or 9. After finding out the value of 1 part, we would assign to A 4 of these parts, to B 3 of these parts, and to C 2 of these parts.

VARIATION 4

Sometimes we deal with a problem in which the salesperson earns a flat salary and a commission. For example:

A broker earned $2000 in one year. He received a flat salary of $100 per month in addition to commission at a rate of 5 percent for anything sold in excess of $15,000. What were his total sales for the year?

Solution

We know that the broker earned $100 per month or $1200 per year as a flat salary. Therefore, out of $2000 earned, $1200 was earned regardless of his sales. That leaves us with $2000 – $1200 or $800 being earned as a result of commissions at a rate of 5 percent on sales over $15,000. To find out how much over $15,000 his sales totaled, we use the triangle method.

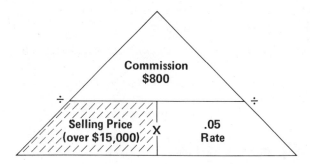

The Selling Price (over $15,000) is $800 ÷ .05 = $16,000. Therefore, the broker sold $16,000 over $15,000 or a total of $31,000 for the year.

VARIATION 5

It is not uncommon to have a situation where a salesperson earns a percent of the total commission earned on a particular sale. For example: a property sells for $21,250. The listing salesperson is to receive $12\frac{1}{2}$ percent of the total 7 percent commission collected on the sale. What was the listing salesperson's share?

Solution

The first step is to derive the total commission that was earned on the sale. We can do this by again using the triangle method.

The Commission Earned on the sale was $21,250 × .07 = $1487.50. The salesperson earned $12\frac{1}{2}$ percent of the total commission on the sale or $12\frac{1}{2}\% \times \$1487.50$.

$$12\frac{1}{2}\% = 12.5\% = .125$$
$$.125 \times \$1487.50 = \$185.94$$

The listing salesperson earned $185.94.

Commission Problems with Solutions

1. A broker was paid $3575 commission on the sale of a $55,000 home. What was the rate of commission?

Solution

Using the basic formula:

$$\text{Selling Price} \times \text{Rate of Commission} = \text{Commission}$$

Selling Price = $55,000
Rate of Commission = ?
Commission = $3575

Putting this information into the triangle

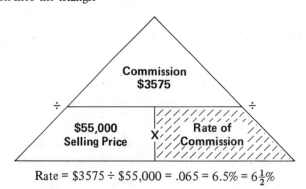

Rate = $3575 ÷ $55,000 = .065 = 6.5% = $6\frac{1}{2}$%

The Rate of Commission was $6\frac{1}{2}$ percent.

2. A broker sells a property worth $33,000. He earns 6 percent commission on the first $15,000 of any sale and $3\frac{1}{2}$ percent commission on anything over $15,000 of any sale. What was his commission?

Solution

The first $15,000 at 6 percent would yield a commission of $15,000 × .06 = $900. The remaining amount is $33,000 - $15,000 = $18,000. Therefore, the remaining commission would be $18.000 × .035 = $630. The Total Commission would be $900 + 630 = $1530.

3. Mr. Mandel earns a 7 percent commission on the first $75,000 of sales and 3 percent commission for all sales over $75,000. He sold houses for $38,000, $60,000, and $45,000.

    (a) How much commission did he earn?
    (b) How much more or less would he earn if he worked on a straight 5 percent commission?

Solution

(a) Mr. Mandel sold homes totaling $143,000. The first $75,000 worth of sales at 7 percent commission yields $75,000 × .07 or $5250 commission. The remaining amount of sales is $143,000 - $75,000 = $68,000. The remaining commission would be $68,000 × 3% = $68,000 × .03 = $2040.
    The Total Commission is $5250 + $2040 = $7290.

(b) Earning commission at a straight 5 percent, we can simply use the triangle method.

Selling Price = $143,000
Rate of Commission = 5% = .05
Commission = ?

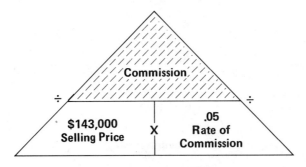

Commission = $143,000 × .05 = $7150

Subtracting the answer (b) from answer (a), we get

$$\$7290 - \$7150 = \$140$$

Mr. Mandel earns $140 less by working on a straight 5 percent commission.

4.   A broker was paid a 6 percent commission on a sale of $47,900. The broker retained 50 percent of the gross commission and paid his sales manager 15 percent of the net, with the balance paid to the salesperson. What was the salesperson's share?

Solution

First we find the total commission by using the basic formula and the triangle method.

Selling Price = $47,000
Rate of Commission = 6%
Commission = ?

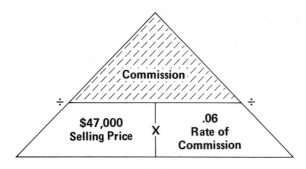

Commission = $47,000 × .06 = $2874

The broker kept 50 percent of the total $2874, or $1437. He paid the sales manager 15 percent of the net or 15 percent of the remaining $1437 = .15 × $1437 = $215.55. The balance or $1437 − $215.55 or $1221.45 went to the salesperson.

5. A broker earns a commission of $750 on the sale of a home. He earns 5 percent commission on the first $10,000 of the sale and 3 percent commission on anything above $10,000. How much did the home sell for?

Solution

We use two triangles to solve the problem. We can find the commission earned on the first $10,000 of the sale by using $10,000 as the selling price and 5 percent for the rate of commission.

The Commission Earned by the first $10,000 of the sale is $10,000 × .05 = $500. Since a total of $750 was earned, we know that the selling price was at least $10,000. Now, looking for the remaining value which earned the broker $250 ($750 – $500), earned at a rate of 3 percent, we again use the triangle method.

The Value of the Home which is greater than $10,000 is $250 ÷ .03 = $8333.33.
The Total Selling Price was $10,000 + 8333.33 = $18,333.33.

6. A broker and salesperson split commission at a ratio of 2:1. How much did each earn on a $35,000 sale, if the total commission earned was a 6 percent rate of commission?

Solution

First we find the total commission to be shared.

$$\text{Selling Price} = \$35,000$$
$$\text{Rate of Commission} = 6\% = .06$$
$$\text{Commission} = ?$$

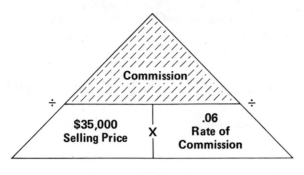

Commission = $35,000 × .06 = $2100

Ratio means part. The broker gets 2 parts and the salesperson gets 1 part, for a total of 3 parts.

$$2100 ÷ 3 = $700$$

Each part is worth $700. The broker gets 2 parts or 2 × $700 or $1400. The salesperson gets 1 part or 1 × $700 = $700.

Practice Commission Problems

1. A house was listed for $60,000 and sold for 87 percent of that amount. The rate of commission was 6 percent and was divided equally between the broker and the salesperson. How much did each get?

2. A house sells for $48,000 with a 6 percent commission going to the broker and salesperson in the ratio of 3:2. How much more than the salesperson did the broker get?

3. Complete the following table:

	COMMISSION RATE	SELLING PRICE	COMMISSION
Broker 1	6%	$25,000	?
Broker 2	?	$32,500	$2600
Broker 3	10%	$43,000	?
Broker 4	5%	?	$1200

4. Calculate the amount of brokerage fee earned by a broker on a property selling for $8564 if his 7 percent commission is paid on the first $5000 of the sale and $3\frac{1}{2}$ percent commission is paid on the remaining amount.

5. If a salesperson earned 4 percent commission on sales for $\frac{1}{3}$ of the year and 6 percent commission on sales for $\frac{2}{3}$ of the year, what was the average rate of commission for the year?

6. A salesperson earns a salary of $150 a month. He earns an additional 4 percent commission on all sales. What were his total yearly sales if he earned $3500 for the year?

7. A broker earns 6 percent commission on the first $8000 of a sale and $3\frac{1}{2}$ percent commission on anything over $8000. The broker received $900 on a particular sale. What was the selling price?

Solutions to Commission Problems

1. The house sold for $60,000 × .87 = $52,200.

Selling Price = $52,200
Rate of Commission = 6% = .06
Commission = ?

Using the triangle method

Commission = $52,200 × .06 = $3132

The broker and the salesperson each get one-half.

$3132 ÷ 2 = $1566

Each gets $1566.

2. First we derive the commission to be shared.

Selling Price = $48,000
Rate of Commission = 6% = .06
Commission = ?

Using the triangle method

Commission = $48,000 × .06 = $2880

The broker and salesperson share commission in the ratio of 3 to 2. Therefore, the broker gets 3 parts and the salesperson gets 2 parts, for a total of 5 parts. To find the value of 1 part, we divide $2880 by 5.

$$\$2880 \div 5 = \$576$$

The broker gets 3 X $576 = $1728
The salesperson gets 2 X $576 = $1152

The broker gets $1728 - $1152, or $576 more than the salesperson. This makes sense, since the broker did get 1 part more than the salesperson and 1 part is worth $576.

3. Broker 1

Selling Price = $25,000
Rate of Commission = 6% = .06
Commission = ?

Commission = $25,000 X .06 = $1500

Broker 2

Selling Price = $32,500
Rate of Commission = ?
Commission = $2600

Rate of Commission = $2600 ÷ $32,500 = .08 = 8%

Broker 3

Selling Price = $43,000
Rate of Commission = .10 = 10%
Commission = ?

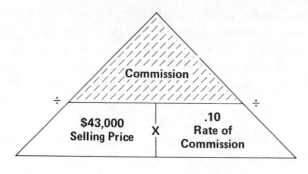

$$\text{Commission} = \$43,000 \times .10 = \$4300$$

Broker 4

Selling Price = ?
Rate of Commission = 5% = .05
Commission = $1200

$$\text{Selling Price} = \$1200 \div .05 = \$24,000$$

Completing the table:

	RATE OF COMMISSION	SELLING PRICE	COMMISSION
Broker 1	6%	$25,000	$1500
Broker 2	8%	$32,500	$2600
Broker 3	10%	$43,000	$4300
Broker 4	5%	$24,000	$1200

4. The first $5000 at 7 percent would yield a Commission of $5000 × .07 = $350. The remaining amount is $8564 – $5000 = $3564. Therefore, the Remaining Commission would be $3564 × $3\frac{1}{2}$% or $3564 × .035 = $124.74. The Total Brokerage Fee is $350 + $124.74 = $474.74.

5. To find the average of any group of numbers, we divide the sum of all the numbers by the amount of numbers we have.

Since we are dealing with thirds, we start with the fact that $\frac{3}{3}$ will equal a year. We will have a total of 3 numbers and then divide by 3 to derive the average. Since 4 percent was earned for $\frac{1}{3}$ of the year, multiplying 4 percent by 1 will give us our first number: $.04 \times 1 = .04$. Six percent was earned for $\frac{2}{3}$ of the year. Multiplying 6 percent by 2 will give us the total of our next two numbers: $.06 \times 2 = .12$. The total of all 3 numbers equals $.04 + .12 = .16$. Now to find the Average Commission divide .16 by 3, which gives us $.05\frac{1}{3}$ or $5\frac{1}{3}\%$.

6.   The salesperson earns $150 a month or $150 × 12 months per year. He earns $1800 per year as his base salary. He earns a total of $3500 for the year. Therefore, $3500 - $1800 or $1700 was earned in commission.

At this point we can use the triangle method.

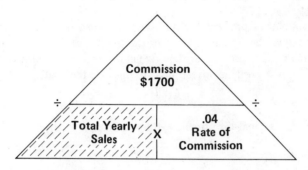

Total Yearly Sales = $1700 ÷ .04 = $42,500

The total yearly sales were $42,500.

7.   Six percent on the first $8000 of sales would earn $.06 \times \$8000$ or $480 commission. The broker earned $900 commission. Therefore, $900 - $480 or $420 commission was earned on sales over $8000 at a $3\frac{1}{2}$ percent commission rate. We can use the triangle to find the balance of the sale price.

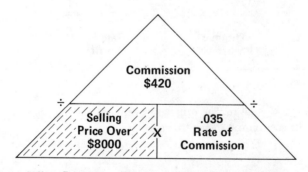

Selling Price over $8000 = $420 ÷ .035 = $12,000

The Total Selling Price was $8000 plus $12,000 = $20,000.

5

PROFIT AND LOSS

PROFIT

In any investment, the amount of profit is the difference between the original investment and the present value. Our basic profit formula will be similar in form to the two types of formulas previously mentioned, the interest and commission formulas. The base sum or the original investment is multiplied by a percent (in this case rate of profit) to yield a portion of the original investment (in this case the profit).

$$\text{Original Investment} \times \text{Rate of Profit} = \text{Profit}$$

We can set up the triangle in the following way to be used for the basic profit problem.

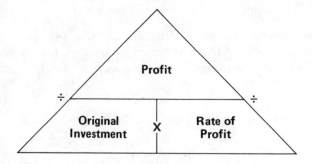

Again, no matter what information is given, the original investment and the rate of profit occupy the bottom spaces of the triangle. The profit goes on top of the triangle.

Sample Basic Profit Problem

If a man invests $5000 and makes a profit of $1000, what is the rate of profit?

We immediately categorize this as a profit problem when we see the key words "invests," "profit," and "rate of profit."

$$\text{Original Investment} = \$5000$$
$$\text{Profit} = \$1000$$
$$\text{Rate of Profit} = ?$$

We put this information into our triangle in the following way

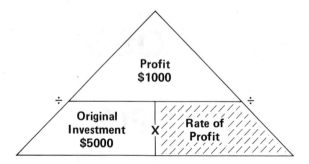

Rate of Profit = $1000 ÷ $5000 = .20 = 20%.

VARIATION 1

The basic profit problem can be varied. Rather than being given the original investment and the profit earned, we might be given the original investment and the current value and then asked to find the rate of profit. For example: If a man invests $10,000, and one year later his investment is worth $12,000, what is the rate of profit?

It is tempting to use $12,000 as the profit. This, of course, is wrong. We first have to subtract the original investment of $10,000 from the current value of $12,000, which would give us a profit of $2000.

$$\text{Original Investment} = \$10,000$$
$$\text{Rate of Profit} = ?$$
$$\text{Profit} = \$2000$$

Using the triangle

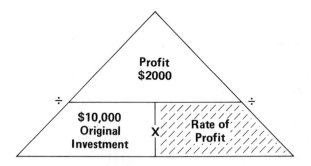

The Rate of Profit = $2000 ÷ $10,000 = .20 = 20%.

VARIATION 2

When the original investment is given and we are also given the rate of profit, we can find the profit and, if asked, the current rent value of the investment. The situation is typified in the following problem:

Mr. Brown bought his home for $25,000. He sold it at a profit of 20 percent. What was the selling price?

Using the triangle we will first derive the profit and then determine the selling price.

Original Investment = $25,000
Rate of Profit = 20% = .20
Profit = ?

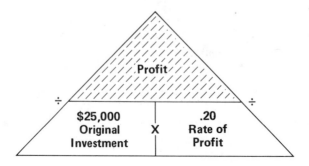

Profit = $25,000 × .20 = $5000.

The Selling Price = Original Investment + Profit or $25,000 + $5000 = $30,000.

> **NOTE**: This type of problem sounds very similar to an appreciation problem. Profit problems and appreciation problems are often interchangeable. The same problem will be dealt with in Chapter 6, using an appreciation formula (problem 2 in Appreciation Problems with Solutions).

If we were given the following problem, we might be tempted to use the profit formula just discussed. This would be incorrect. Let's look at the problem:

Mr. Smith bought a home in 1975. In 1977 he sold it for $30,000, which represented a 25 percent profit. What was the original investment?

The key words "profit" and "original investment" seem to dictate that we use the profit formula. We would need two out of the three unknowns in order to use our formula. We know the rate of profit is 25 percent. However, we do not know and have no way of finding out the original investment or the profit. We do not have enough information. We would have to use the appreciation formula which will be presented later.

In summary, profit and appreciation problems are interchangeable if we are given the original investment or the actual amount of profit. If we are not given either of these, we must use the appreciation formula.

VARIATION 3

We are sometimes given the original investment in the form of a list of expenses. For example:

Mrs. Jones bought a home for $15,000 and made improvements on the home totalling $2200. What percent profit did she make upon selling the home for $19,780?

The Original Investment would be $15,000 + $2200 = $17,200. The house sold for $19,780. Therefore, the Profit was $19,780 – $17,200 = $2580.

Original Investment = $17,200
Rate of Profit = ?
Profit = $2580

Using the triangle

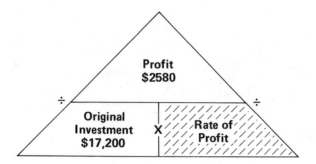

Rate of Profit = $2580 ÷ $17,200 = .15 = 15%.

LOSS

Loss problems are similar to profit problems with the obvious difference that we end up with less money than we had originally. The loss is the difference between the original investment and the specified end result. It is important to remember that you must consider the loss in terms of the original investment.

Our basic formula will have the original investment as the base sum, multiplied by a percent (in this case, the rate of loss), to yield a portion of the original investment (in this case, the loss).

$$\text{Original Investment} \times \text{Rate of Loss} = \text{Loss}$$

We can set up the triangle in the following way to be used for the basic loss problem.

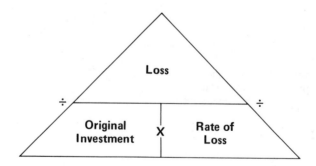

Sample Basic Loss Problem

Five months after investing $1000, a man had lost $400 of this original investment. What was the rate of loss?

$$\text{Original Investment} = \$1000$$
$$\text{Rate of Loss} = ?$$
$$\text{Loss} = \$400$$

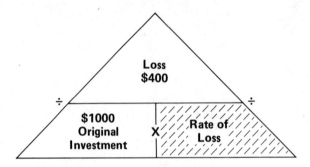

Rate of Loss = $400 ÷ $1000 = .40 = 40%.

VARIATION 1

The basic loss problem can be varied by being given the original investment and the end result and then asked to find the rate of loss. We therefore have the additional task of finding the loss in order to begin the problem. The loss is found by subtracting the end result from the original investment. For example:

When selling her home, Mrs. Baker agreed to sell her antique living room set for $600. She had originally purchased the set for $750. What percent loss did she suffer?

$$\text{Original Investment} = \$750$$
$$\text{Loss} = \$750 - \$600 = \$150$$
$$\text{Rate of Loss} = ?$$

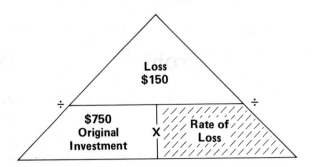

Rate of Loss = $150 ÷ 750 = .20 = 20%.

VARIATION 2

Another variation occurs when we are given the original investment, the rate of loss, and are required to find the loss or the current value of the investment. For example:

A man invests $2000. He suffers a loss at the rate of 15 percent. What is the current value of his investment?

$$\text{Original Investment} = \$2000$$
$$\text{Rate of Loss} = 15\%$$
$$\text{Loss} = ?$$

Using the triangle

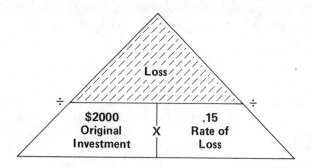

Loss = $2000 × .5 = $300.

If he started with a $2000 investment and lost $300, the Current Value of the investment must be $2000 – $300 = $1700.

> **NOTE**: Just as profit problems and appreciation problems can sometimes be interchanged, the same holds true for loss and depreciation problems. Variation 2 will be solved again in Chapter 6 using the depreciation formula (problem 6 in Depreciation Problems with Solutions).

If we are given the following problem, we might be tempted to use the loss formula just discussed. This would be incorrect. Let's look at the problem:

Mr. Haley bought an apartment building in 1975. One year later it was worth $100,000, which represented a loss of 25 percent. What was the original investment?

To use the loss formula, we would have to know two out of three of the unknowns. However, we have neither the original investment nor the loss. Therefore, it would be impossible to find the original investment using this formula. For this problem, we would have to use the depreciation formula as described in Chapter 6.

Depreciation and loss problems are interchangeable if we are given the original investment or the amount of loss. If we are not given either of these, we must use the depreciation formula.

Profit and Loss Problems with Solutions

1.   If an original investment of $120,000 brings a profit of $1200, what is the percent of profit?

Solution

Original investment = $120,000
Rate of Profit = ?
Profit = $1200

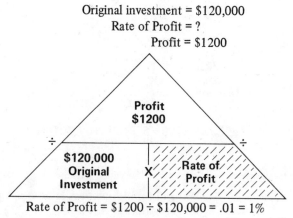

Rate of Profit = $1200 ÷ $120,000 = .01 = 1%

The percent of profit is 1%.

2.   Mrs. Marshall bought a house for $18,000 and made improvements totalling $3000. What percent profit did she make upon selling the house for $24,000?

Solution

Original Investment = $18,000 + $3000 = $21,000
Rate of Profit = ?
Profit = $24,000 - $21,000 = $3000

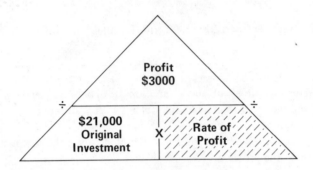

Rate of Profit = $3000 ÷ $21,000 = .142 = 14.2% = 14%

She made a 14 percent profit.

3.   Mrs. Harris invests $2000 and 1 year later her investment is worth only $1800. What is the rate of loss?

Solution

Original Investment = $2000
Rate of Loss = ?
Loss = $2000 - $1800 = $200

Rate of Loss = $200 ÷ $2000 = .10 = 10%

Her rate of loss is 10 percent.

4.   Mrs. Bearman bought a property for $32,000 and sold it one year later at a 4 percent loss. What was the selling price?

Solution

Original Investment = $32,000
Rate of Loss = 4%
Loss = ?

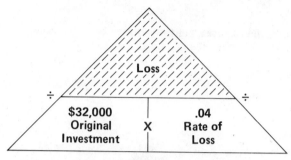

Loss = $32,000 × .04 = $1280
Selling Price = $32,000 − $1280 = $30,720

The selling price was $30,720.

5. Mrs. Lewin bought a piece of property 5 years ago for $55,000 and sold if for a 25 percent profit. How much did she sell it for?

Solution

Original Investment = $55,000
Rate of Profit = 25% = .25
Profit = ?

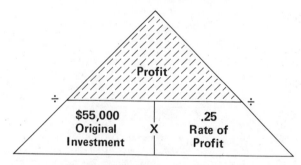

Profit = $55,000 × .25 = $13,750
Selling Price = $55,000 + $13,750 = $68,750

She sold it for $68,750.

Practice Profit and Loss Problems

1. A man invests $4000 in a lot. A year later the lot is worth only $2800. What is the rate of loss?

2. Mrs. Lerner makes 40 percent profit on her investment. Her profit is $15,000. What was her original investment?

3. If you bought a house for the listed price less 15 percent and sold it for the listed price, what percent profit would you make?

Solutions to Profit and Loss Problems

1.

Original Investment = $4000
Rate of Loss = ?
Loss = $4000 – $2800 = $1200

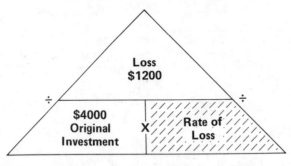

Rate of Loss = $1200 ÷ $4000 = .30 = 30%

The rate of loss is 30 percent.

2.

Original Investment = ?
Rate of Profit = 40% = .40
Profit = $15,000

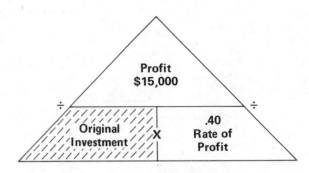

Original Investment = $15,000 ÷ .40 = $37,500

The original investment was $37,500.

3. Choose any list price. Choosing a list price of $10,000, the property was bought at 15 percent less than the list price of $10,000.

15% of $10,000 = .15 × $10,000 = $1500

Therefore, the Original Investment = $8500 ($10,000 – $1500). If the Selling Price was $10,000 (the list price), then the Profit is $10,000 – $8500 = $1500.

Original Investment = $8500
Rate of Profit = ?
Profit = $1500

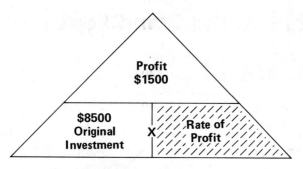

Rate of Profit = $1500 ÷ $8500 = .176 = .18 = 18%

6

APPRECIATION AND DEPRECIATION

In the buying and selling of real estate, we often speak about the appreciation and depreciation of the value of property; appreciation meaning that the original value has increased, depreciation meaning that the original value has decreased. The percent of appreciation or depreciation is always with respect to the original price, leaving us with a higher or lower value in the present.

APPRECIATION

Suppose a property were to appreciate 20 percent. We know it is presently worth at least the same as or 100 percent of its original value. In fact, its present price is 100 percent plus 20 percent or 120 percent of its original price. If a property were to appreciate 35 percent, its present price would be at least 100 percent of its original price, plus an additional 35 percent or 135 percent of its original value. If a property appreciates 50 percent, its present price would be 150 percent of its original price. Of course, the rate of appreciation varies, depending upon the particular problem. To arrive at a general formula, let's say a property appreciates A percent. The present price would be 100 and A percent of its original price. This gives us the following appreciation formula:

Present Price = (100 + A)% of the Original Price

or

Present Price = (100 + A)% × Original Price

Since (100 + A)% is multiplied by the original price to yield the present price, we can put the formula into the triangle as follows

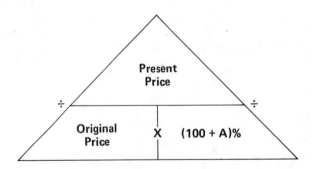

Sample Basic Appreciation Problem

If a property is presently valued at $20,000 after having appreciated 15 percent in value during the last ten years, what was the original value?

Present Price = $20,000
(100 + A)% = 115% = 1.15
Original Price = ?

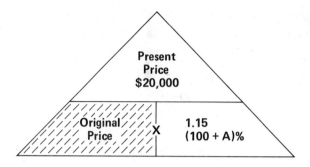

Original Price = $20,000 ÷ 1.15 = $17,391.30.

NOTE: In the above problem, one might be tempted to use the fact that the property appreciated in value during a 10 year period. In this basic problem, the 10 years is just part of the story. We are not being told that the property appreciated on the average at a particular rate for 10 years. We are merely being given extra information. It is not to be used. In the following variation this is not the case.

VARIATION 1

If a property is presently valued at $22,000, having appreciated on the average of $2\frac{1}{2}$ percent per year for the last 10 years, what was the value 10 years ago?

In this case, the 10 year period of time is very significant. We are told that the property appreciates on the average of $2\frac{1}{2}$ percent each year for 10 years. We must now multiply $2\frac{1}{2}$ by 10 to give us the fact that over the 10 year period the property appreciated 25 percent. We now proceed in the same way as the basic appreciation problem.

Present Price = $22,000
(100 + A)% = (100 + 25)% = 125% = 1.25
Original Price = ?

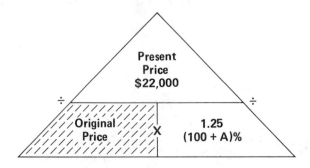

Original Price = $22,000 ÷ 1.25 = $17,600.

VARIATION 2

If the present price of an 8 year old home is established at $35,000 and the original cost was $26,600, what was the rate of appreciation?

NOTE: The appreciation formula calls for (100 + A)%. We are actually looking for A%. First, we find (100 + A)% by using the triangle method and then look for just A%.

Original Price = $26,600
(100 + A)% = ?
Present Price = $35,000

(100 + A)% = $35,000 ÷ $26,600 = 1.32 = 132%

The pitfall is right here. One might think that the property appreciated 132 percent in value. Again, 132 percent represents (100 + A)%. Therefore, A percent is merely the difference between 100 percent and 132 percent or 32 percent. The property appreciated 32 percent in value.

VARIATION 3

A house worth $15,000 appreciated at a rate of 10 percent each year over the previous year's value. What was the property worth at the beginning of the third year?

This problem has two possible pitfalls. First, the property appreciates 10 percent each year. Therefore, each year the 10 percent appreciation rate is multiplied by a new number. Second, the value of the property at the beginning of the third year is the same as the value at the end of the second. If we find the value of the property by the end of the first year and then again by the end of the second year, we will arrive at our answer.

Using the appreciation formula and two triangles is the best approach to solving our problem.

Original Price (beginning of first year) = $15,000
(100 + A)% = 110% = 1.10
Present Price (end of first year) = ?

Present Price or Value at the end of the first year = $15,000 × 1.10 = $16,500.

The value at the end of the first year is the same as the value at the beginning of the second year. The value at the beginning of the second year = $16,500. This now becomes our new original price. We start the process again for the second time.

Original Price (beginning second year) = $16,500
(100 + A)% = 110% = 1.10
Present Price (end of second year) = ?

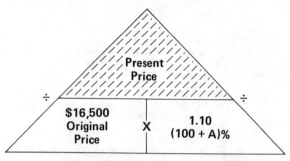

Present Price (end of second year) = $16,500 × 1.10 = $18,150. The property is worth $18,150 at the end of the second year, which is the same as the beginning of the third year.

NOTE: Had we been told that the property appreciated on the average of 10 percent each year for 2 years, we would have had a problem such as variation 1 and simply multiplied 10 percent by 2 to give us an appreciation rate of 20 percent. This was not the case in this problem. We might start suspecting this type of compound situation when we are dealing with just a few years worth of appreciation. It is doubtful one would be required to work out 10 or 15 separate computations; two or three is not unreasonable.

Appreciation Problems with Solutions

1. A property is presently valued at $25,000 after having appreciated 20 percent in value over the last ten years. What was the original value?

Solution

Original Price = ?
(100 + A)% = (100 + 20)% = 120% = 1.20
Present Price = $25,000

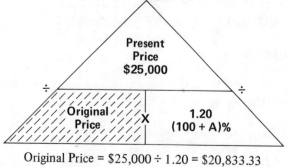

Original Price = $25,000 ÷ 1.20 = $20,833.33

The original value was $20,833.33.

2. Mr. Brown bought his home for $25,000. He sold it at a 20 percent profit. What was the selling price?

Solution

Original Price = $25,000
(100 + A)% = 120% = 1.20
Present Price = ?

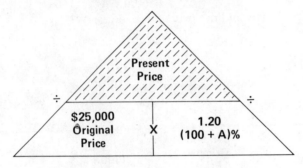

Present Price = $25,000 × 1.20 = $30,000
Selling Price = $30,000

The selling price was $30,000.

3.　If a home's current appraisal value of $42,000 is $112\frac{1}{2}$ percent of the original cost, what is the original cost?

Solution

Original Price = ?
(100 + A)% = $112\frac{1}{2}$% = 112.5% = 1.125
Present Price = $42,000

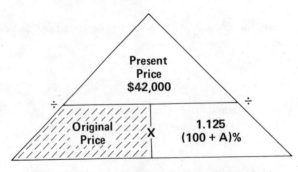

Original Price = $42,000 ÷ 1.125 = $37,333.33

The original cost was $37,333.33.

4.　If a property is presently valued at $18,800 having appreciated on the average of 2 percent each year for the last $7\frac{1}{2}$ years, what was the value $7\frac{1}{2}$ years ago?

Solution

We are told the property appreciated on the average of 2 percent each year for $7\frac{1}{2}$ years. To find the percent of appreciation for $7\frac{1}{2}$ years, we multiply 2% × $7\frac{1}{2}$ = 2% × 7.5 = 15%.

Original Price = ?
(100 + A)% = (100 + 15)% = 1.15
Present Price = $18,800

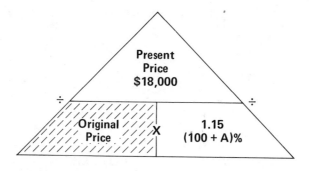

Original Price = $18,800 ÷ 1.15 = $16,347.83

The price $7\frac{1}{2}$ years ago was $16,347.83.

5.   A lot's current appraisal value is $15,000. Six years ago its original value was $9000. Find the average rate of appreciation per year.

Solution

Present Price = $15,000
(100 + A)% = ?
Original Price = $9000

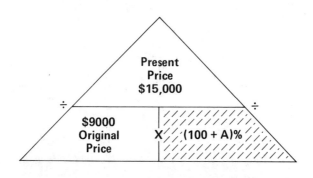

(100 + A)% = $15,000 ÷ $9000 = 1.67 = 167%

Since (100 + A)% = 167%, then A = 67%. If the property appreciated a total of 67 percent over a 6 year period, the average rate of appreciation per year would be

$$67\% \div 6 = 11\frac{1}{6}\% \text{ per year.}$$

The average rate of appreciation per year is $11\frac{1}{6}\%$.

6.   A property is worth $3000. The annual appreciation rate is 8 percent over the previous year's value. How much would the lot be worth in 2 years?

Solution

Original Price (beginning first year) = $3000
(100 + A)% = 108% = 1.08
Present Price (end of first year) = ?

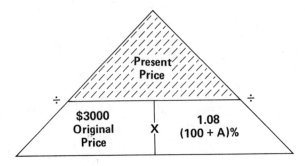

Present Price or Value at the end of the first year = $3000 × 1.08 = $3240

The value at the beginning of the second year = $3240. This now becomes our original price.

Original Price (beginning second year) = $3240
(100 + A)% = 108% = 1.08
Present Price (end of second year) = ?

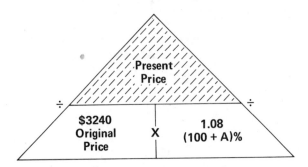

Present Price (end of second year) = $3240 × 1.08 = $3499.20

At the end of the 2 years, the property would be worth $3499.20.

DEPRECIATION

If a property depreciated 20 percent in value, it would no longer be worth the same as, or 100 percent of, its original value. It would be worth 100 percent − 20 percent or 80 percent of its original value. If a property depreciated 40 percent, it would now be worth 100 percent − 40 percent or 60 percent of its original value. If a property were to depreciate 35 percent it would be worth 100 percent − 35 percent or 65 percent of its original value. To arrive at a general formula, let's say a property depreciates D percent. The present price would be (100 − D)% of its original price. This gives us the following formula:

Present Price = (100 − D)% of Original Price
or
Present Price = (100 − D)% × Original Price

Since (100 – D)% is multiplied by the original price to yield the present price, we can put the formula into the triangle as follows

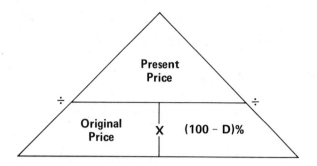

Sample Basic Depreciation Problem

If a property is currently worth $25,000 after having depreciated 33 percent in value over the last 8 years, what was the original price?

Present Price = $25,000
(100 – D)% = (100 – 33)% = 67%
Original Price = ?

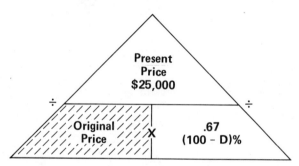

Original Price = $25,000 ÷ .67 = $37,313.43.

NOTE: In the above problem, the fact that the property depreciated a total of 33 percent over an 8 year period is just part of the story and is not to be used. We do not need this fact to figure out the rate of depreciation. We have already been given enough information to solve our problem. In the following variation, this is not the case.

VARIATION 1

A property is worth $15,000 when purchased. It continues to depreciate on the average of 2 percent per year for the next 6 years. What is the property worth at the end of these 6 years?

In this problem, we must use the 6 year figure given. We are told that the property depreciates on an average of 2 percent per year for 6 years or a total of 12 percent in all. We now proceed with this information in the usual way.

Present Price = ?
(100 – D)% = (100 – 12)% = 88%
Original Price = $15,000

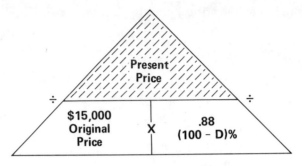

Present Price = $15,000 × .88 = $13,200.

VARIATION 2

If the present value of a home is $50,000 and the original value was $60,000, what was the rate of depreciation?

NOTE: The depreciation formula calls for (100 – D)%. We are actually looking for D percent. First we find (100 – D)% by using the triangle method and then look for just D.

Original Price = $60,000
(100 – D)% = ?
Present Price = $50,000

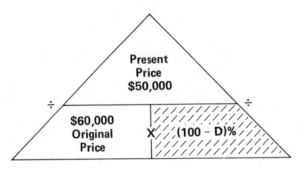

(100 – D)% = $50,000 ÷ $60,000 = .83 = 83%.

There are pitfalls here. If (100 – D)% = 83%, this does not mean that the property depreciated 83 percent. What 83 percent represents is the difference between 100 percent and D percent. Therefore, D percent is 17 percent. The Rate of Depreciation which we are looking for is 17 percent.

VARIATION 3

A $2000 property depreciates at a rate of 5 percent each year. How much is it worth at the beginning of the fourth year?

This problem has two possible pitfalls. First, we must realize that the property depreciated 5 percent each year. Therefore, each year the 5 percent depreciation rate is multiplying a new number. Second, the value of the property at the beginning of the fourth year is the same as the value at the end of the third year. Now we have three separate computations to perform. If we find the property's value at the end of the first year, then by the end of the second year, then by the end of the third year, we will have the value for the beginning of the fourth year. We will have arrived at our solution.

Original Price (beginning first year) = $2000
$$(100 - D)\% = (100 - 5)\% = 95\%$$
Present Price (end of first year) = ?

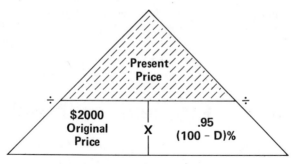

Present Price (end of first year) = $2000 × .95 = $1900.

The property is worth $1900 by the end of the first year, which is the same as the beginning of the second year. Now we begin again.

Original Price (beginning second year) = $1900
$$(100 - D)\% = (100 - 5)\% = 95\%$$
Present Price (end of second year) = ?

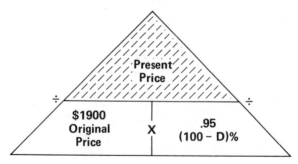

Present Price (end of second year) = $1900 × .95 = $1805.

The property is worth $1805 by the end of the second year, which is the same as the beginning of the third year. Now we begin once more.

Original Price (beginning third year) = $1805
$$(100 - D)\% = (100 - 5)\% = 95\%$$
Present Price (end of third year) = ?

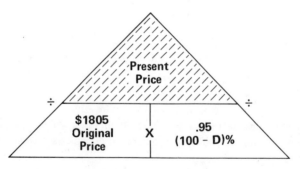

Present Price (end third year) = $1805 × .95 = $1714.75.

The property is worth $1714.75 by the end of the third year, which is the same as its value at the beginning of the fourth year.

The property is worth $1714.75 by the beginning of the fourth year.

NOTE: It would seem unlikely that one would be asked to perform the above procedure as many as 5 or 6 times. Therefore, one should not expect to use this compound procedure if a property is depreciating for more than 5 years.

Depreciation Problems with Solutions

1. The value of a farm house is $16,000 after having depreciated 32 percent in value during the last 7 years. What was the original value?

Solution

Original Price = ?
(100 − D)% = (100 − 32)% = 68% = .68
Present Price = $16,000

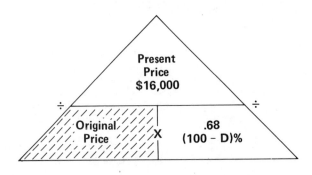

Original Price = $16,000 ÷ .68 = $23,529.41

The original value was $23,529.41.

2. A property valued at $12,000 depreciated 5 percent in value every year. What is its value at the beginning of the third year?

Solution

We are told the value of the house depreciates 5 percent each year. Finding the value at the beginning of the third year is the same as finding its value at the end of the second year. We must work out 2 separate computations.

NOTE: We have not been told the property decreased in value on the average of 5 percent each year. In that case, we would simply multiply 5 percent by 2 and use 10 percent as our total rate of depreciation.

Original Price (beginning first year) = $12,000

$$(100 - D)\% = (100 - 5)\% = 95\% = .95$$

Present Price (end of first year) = ?

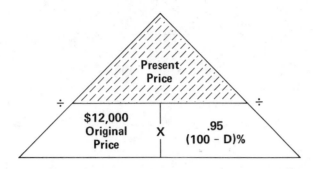

Present Price (end of first year) = $12,000 × .95 = $11,400

The property is worth $11,400 by the end of the first year, which is the same as the value at the beginning of the second year. We now begin the process again.

Original Price (beginning of the second year) = $11,400

$$(100 - D)\% = (100 - 5)\% = 95\% = .95$$

Present Price (end of second year) = ?

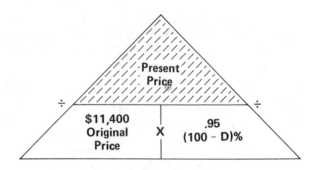

Present Price (end of second year) = $11,400 × .95 = $10,830

The value of the property at the end of the second year is $10,830, which is the same as the value at the beginning of the third year.

The property is worth $10,830 by the beginning of the third year.

3. If the original cost of a 5 year old house was $18,000, what is the present value of the house if the rate of depreciation is $12\frac{1}{2}$ percent?

Solution

Original Price = $18,000

$$(100 - D)\% = (100 - 12\tfrac{1}{2})\% = 87\tfrac{1}{2}\% = .875$$

Present Price = ?

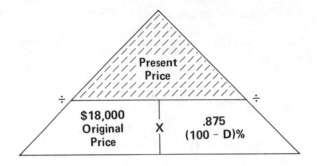

Present Price = $18,000 × .875 = $15,750

The value of the house is $15,750.

4. A home and lot were valued at $13,800 six years ago. Of this price, it was estimated that the lot carried a
    a value of $4500 when purchased. Assuming a depreciation rate of 24 percent on the home and an apprecia-
    tion rate of 20 percent on the lot, what is the total value of the property today?

Solution

If the original value of the lot was $4500, then the original value of the home was $13,800 − $4500 = $9300.
We can work on the depreciation of the home and the appreciation of the lot separately.

<u>Home</u>

Original Value = $9300
(100 − D)% = (100 − 24)% = 76% = .76
Present Price = ?

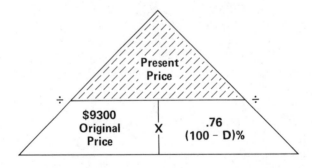

Present Price of the Home = $9300 × .76 = $7068

<u>Lot</u>

Original Price = $4500
(100 + A)% = (100 + 20)% = 120% = 1.20
Present Price = ?

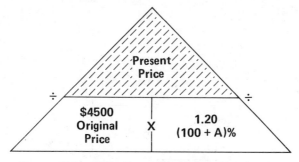

Present Price of the Lot = $4500 × 1.20 = $5400

Present Price of the Home + Present Price of the Lot = $7068 + $5400 = $12,468

The total value of the property is $12,468.

5. A home is worth $42,000 after having depreciated in value over the last 7 years. If its original value is $45,000, find the average rate of depreciation per year.

Solution

Original Price = $4500
$(100 - D)\% = ?$
Present Price = $42,000

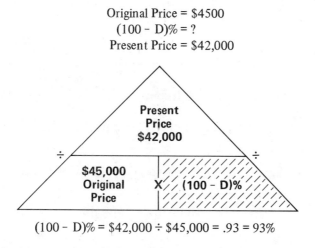

$(100 - D)\% = \$42,000 \div \$45,000 = .93 = 93\%$

If $(100 - D)\% = 93\%$ then $D\% = 7\%$. The Average Rate of Depreciation over a 7 year period is $7\% \div 7 = 1\%$ per year.

The property depreciates on the average of 1 percent per year.

6. A man invests $2000. He suffers a loss at the rate of 15 percent. What is the current value of his investment?

Solution

Original Price = $2000
$(100 - D)\% = (100 - 15)\% = 85\%$
Present price = ?

Using the triangle

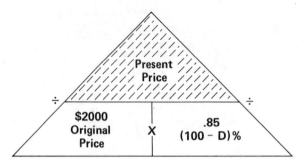

Present price = $2000 × .85 = $1700.

Practice Appreciation Problems

1. If the value of a farm house is presently $22,000, having appreciated on the average of $2\frac{1}{2}$ percent for each year for the first 10 years, what was the value 10 years ago?

2. An owner sold his property for $24,000, the property having appreciated 10 percent in value. What was the original cost?

3. If the present value of a 5 year old house is established at $32,000 and the original cost was $24,000, what was the average yearly rate of appreciation?

4. The annual appreciation rate of a house is 6 percent over the previous year's value. If a house is worth $35,000 originally, how much would it be worth after 3 years?

5. A home is presently worth $65,000, which is 150 percent of its original cost. Find the original cost.

Solutions to Appreciation Problems

1. Since the farm house appreciated on the average of $2\frac{1}{2}$ percent a year, each year for 10 years, A = $2\frac{1}{2}$% × 10 = 2.5% × 10 = 25%.

Original Price = ?
    (100 + A)% = (100 + 25)% = 125%
Present Price = $22,000

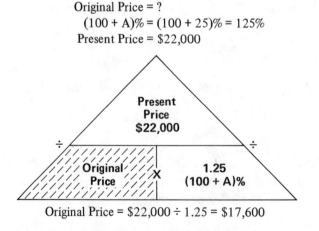

Original Price = $22,000 ÷ 1.25 = $17,600

The Original Price is $17,600.

2.

Original Price = ?
(100 + A)% = 110% = 1.10
Present Price = $24,000

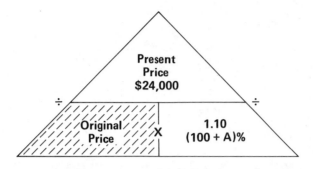

Original Price = $24,000 ÷ 1.10 = $21,818.18

The Original Price is $21,818.18.

3.

Original Price = $24,000
(100 + A)% = ?
Present Price = $32,000

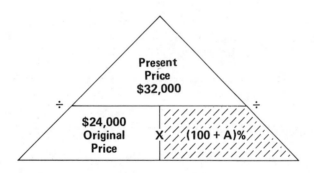

(100 + A)% = $32,000 ÷ $24,000 = 1.33 = 133%

If (100 + A)% = 133% then A = 33%. To find the average rate of appreciation per year for 5 years, we divide 33 percent by 5.

$$33\% \div 5 = 6\tfrac{3}{5}\%$$

The Average Yearly Rate of Appreciation = $6\tfrac{3}{5}\%$.

4. We are told the value of the house increases by 6 percent each year over the previous year's value. To find its worth in three years, we must work out 3 separate computations.

    NOTE: (a) We have not been told the property increased in value on the average of 6 percent each year for 3 years. In that case, we would simply multiply 3 × 6% to give us 18% as the appreciation rate.

    (b) We have not been told that the property appreciated 6 percent over a 3 year period or 6 percent would be our appreciation rate.

Original Price (beginning of first year) = $35,000

(100 + A)% = 106% = 1.06

Present Price (end of first year) = ?

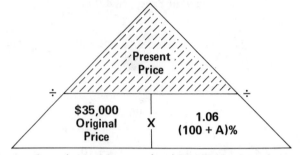

Present Price (end of first year) = $35,000 × 1.06 = $37,100

The value of the property at the beginning of the second year is now $37,100, which is our new original price.

Original Price (beginning of second year) = $37,000

(100 + A)% = 106% = 1.06

Present Price (end of second year) = ?

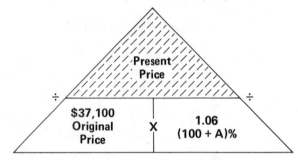

Present Price (end of second year) = $37,100 × 1.06 = $39,326

The value of the property at the beginning of the third year is now $39,326, our new original price.

Original Price (beginning of third year) = $39,326 × 1.06 = $41,686. The property is worth $41,686 after three years.

5.

Original Price = ?

(100 + A)% = 150% = 1.50

Present Price = $65,000

Original Price = $65,000 ÷ 1.50 = $43,333.33

The original cost was $43,333.33.

Practice Depreciation Problems

1. A house bought for $20,000 depreciated at the rate of 6 percent over the previous year's value. What is it worth at the end of the second year?

2. A property is currently appraised for $33,000 after having depreciated 8 percent over a 5 year period. What was the original price?

3. Mrs. Lerner buys a property for $18,000. In 3 years it is worth $12,000. Find the average rate of depreciation per year.

4. A property depreciates on the average of 8 percent per year for 5 years. What is the present price if the original value was $25,000?

Solutions to Depreciation Problems

1.

Original Price (beginning of first year) = $20,000
(100 − D)% = (100 − 6)% = 94%
Present Price (end of first year) = ?

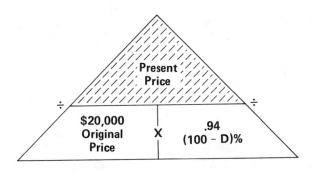

Present Price (end of first year) = $20,000 × .94 = $18,800

The value at the end of the first year or the beginning of the second year is $18,800. Now we begin again.

Original Price (beginning of second year) = $18,800
(100 − D)% = (100 − 6)% = 94%
Present Price (end of second year) = $18,800 × .94 = $17,672

The property is worth $17,672 by the end of the second year.

2.

Original Price = ?
(100 − D)% = (100 − 8)% = 92%
Present Price = $33,000

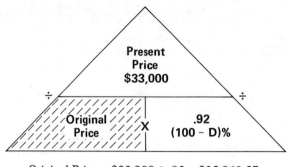

Original Price = $33,000 ÷ .92 = $35,869.57

The property is originally worth $35,869.57.

3.

Original Price = $18,000
(100 – D)% = ?
Present Price = $12,000

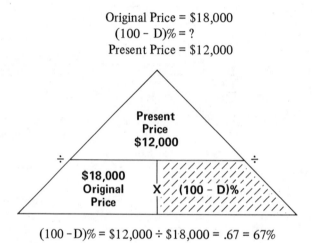

(100 – D)% = $12,000 ÷ $18,000 = .67 = 67%

The Average Rate of Depreciation per year is 33 percent ÷ 3 = 11%. The property depreciates on the average of 11 percent per year.

4.   Since we are told that the property depreciated on the average of 8 percent each year for 5 years, we know the rate of depreciation over the 5 year period would be 8% × 5 = 40%. Therefore, D% = 40% and (100 – D)% = (100 – 40)% = 60%.

Original Price = $25,000
(100 – D)% = (100 – 40)% = 60%
Present Price = ?

Present Price = $25,000 × .60 = $15,000

The present price is $15,000.

7

NET PROFIT

There are two basic types of net profit problems. In the first type we begin with a gross income; that is all of the money which is collected during a particular time period by a particular business or private party. The net profit is simply the gross income less all expenses incurred within that specific time period. The formula we can use is as follows:

$$\text{Net Profit} = \text{Gross Income} - \text{Expenses}$$

We can represent this formula by using a circle diagram as a visual aid.

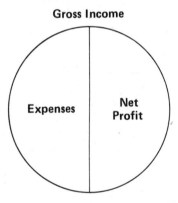

This circle will represent 100 percent of the gross income. Once we shave away expenses we are left with our net profit.

NOTE: (1) This first type of net profit problem involves no commission to a broker or salesperson. (2) We do not use the triangle method with this formula since we do not have the two unknowns multiplied to give us a third.

Sample Basic Net Profit Problem (Type 1)

A man buys 2 lots for $9000 each and divides them into 3 lots, which were sold for $7500 each. What was his net profit?

Net Profit = Gross Income - Expenses
Gross Income = 3 X $7500 = $22,500
Expenses = 2 X $9000 = $18,000

This circle represents $22,500

Net Profit = $22,500 - $18,000 = $4500.

VARIATION 1

We are often asked to compare net profits in two different situations. We proceed by using the same formula in each option and then find the difference between the net profits. The following is an example:

In an apartment house with 12 apartments, rent is $100 per month with utilities (that is, the landlord pays for the utilities). If utilities cost an average of $1944 per year for the apartment house, how much more is the owner netting annually than if he rented the apartment for $82.50 per month, without utilities?

Option 1

In option 1, we first multiply the rental of $100 per month by 12 (since there are 12 apartments) to find the gross income per month and then multiply again by 12 (12 months in a year) to find the annual gross income.

Therefore, the gross income in option 1 is:

$$\$100 \times 12 = \$1200 \text{ per month}$$
$$\$1200 \times 12 = \$14{,}400 \text{ per year}$$

The Gross Income in Option 1 is $14,400.

Expenses = $1944 per year. Using the circle diagram

We let this circle represent the gross income of $14,400.

Net Profit in Option 1 = Gross Income - Expenses =
$14,400 - $1944 = $12,456.

Option 2

In option 2, we first multiply the rental of $82.50 per month by 12 (since there are 12 apartments) to find the gross income per month and then multiply again by 12 (12 months in a year) to find the annual gross income. Therefore, the gross income in option 2 is:

$$\$82.50 \times 12 = \$990 \text{ per month}$$
$$\$990 \times 12 = \$11,800 \text{ per year}$$

The Gross Income in Option 2 is $11,800.
  Expenses = 0 (theoretically). Using the circle diagram

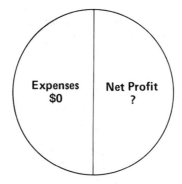

We let this circle represent the gross income of $11,800.

Net Profit in Option 2 = Gross Income – Expenses =
$$\$11,800 - 0 = \$11,800.$$

The Net Profit in Option 1 is $12,456, while the Net Profit in Option 2 is $11,800. The difference is $12,456 – $11,800 = $576 more netted with Option 1.

The second type of net profit problem deals with the sale of real estate in which we are involved with a commission paid to a broker. We can use a circle diagram to describe this type of net profit problem as well. We will let the circle represent 100 percent of the selling price.

Let's suppose the broker will get 6 percent of the selling price. We can simply shave away that 6 percent right off the circle, leaving only 94 percent of the selling price going to the owner of the home. This is depicted in the diagram on the next page.

This remaining 94 percent of the selling price should take into account all expenses, including original price (if given), and a **net profit** which the seller would like to realize. Therefore, our diagram should look like this.

Seller's share of the selling price.

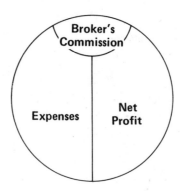

Sample Net Profit Problem (Type 2)

Mr. Smith sold his home for $40,000, which he had originally purchased for $25,000. A $1000 sidewalk assessment has been levied against his property. What was his net profit after paying a broker a 6 percent sales commission?

Using this information in the circle diagram, we have the following

94% of Selling Price (40,000).

94% of $40,000 = .94 × $40,000 = $37,600.

We now have the following

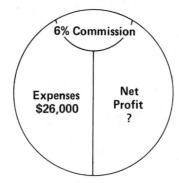

37,600

Looking at our diagram, we can see that if we subtract $26,000 in expenses from the $37,600 (which represents 94 percent of the selling price), we are left with a Net Profit of $37,600 - $26,000 = $11,600.

VARIATION 2

A problem becomes a bit more complicated when we do not know the selling price and we are given the expenses, net profit, and rate of commission. For example:

If an owner makes a net profit of $8490 after purchasing a property for $25,000, and after paying a broker 4 percent commission, what must the selling price be?

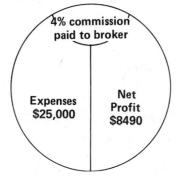

96% of Selling Price
or
.96 X S.P.

We can see that the circle which has a 4 percent broker's commission shaved off the top represents 96 percent of the selling price, which is unknown to us. Adding together the expenses and the net profit, we get $25,000 + $8490 = $33,490. Therefore, 96 percent of the Selling Price = $33,490.

Since .96 X Selling Price = $33,490 (two numbers multiplied to yield a third), we can use the triangle method to solve for the selling price.

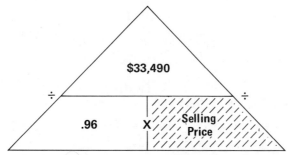

Selling Price = $33,490 ÷ .96 = $34,885.42.

Net Profit Problems with Solutions

1.   A property manager is in charge of renting 5 apartments, each renting at $150 per month. In a year's time the owner incurs expenses for improvements of $2000. What is the owner's net profit that year?

Solution

We know that Net Profit = Gross Income − Expenses.

$$\text{Gross Income} = \$150 \times 5 = \$750 \text{ per month}$$
$$\$750 \times 12 = \$9000 \text{ per year}$$
$$\text{Expenses} = \$2000$$

Using the circle diagram

We let this circle represent a gross income of $9000.

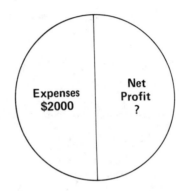

$$\text{Net Profit} = \$9000 - \$2000 = \$7000$$

The Net Profit is $7000.

2.   A builder buys 10 acres of land at $1000 per acre. On this land, he builds 10 houses at a cost of $18,000 each. Each home is sold for $25,000. What is the builder's net profit?

Solution

Gross Income = $25,000 × 10 = $250,000

Expenses = $1000 × 10 for the land + $18,000 × 10 for the houses = $10,000 + $180,000 = $190,000

Now using the circle diagram

We let this circle represent the gross income of $250,000.

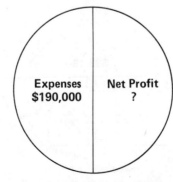

Net Profit = $250,000 − $190,000 = $60,000

The Net Profit is $60,000.

3. In listing a home, the owner tells you that he must net $4000 after paying off his $16,200 mortgage and a paving lien of $245. Your commission is to be 6 percent. What is the listed price?

Solution

$$\text{Expenses} = \$16,200 + \$245 = \$16,445$$
$$\text{Net Profit} = \$4000$$

Using the circle diagram

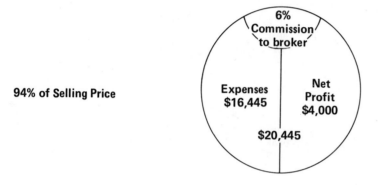

$$94\% \text{ of the Selling Price must} = \$20,445$$
$$.94 \times \text{S. P.} = \$20,445$$

Now using the triangle

$$\text{Selling Price} = \$20,445 \div .94 = \$21,750$$

The Selling Price is $21,750.

4. A house sells for $42,000. The original purchase price is $29,000. Improvements total $4500. If the broker gets 7 percent commission for selling the house, find the owner's net profit.

Solution

$$\text{Selling Price} = \$42,000$$
$$\text{Expenses} = \$29,000 + \$4500 = \$33,500$$
$$\text{Net Profit} = ?$$

Using the circle diagram

93% of $42,000

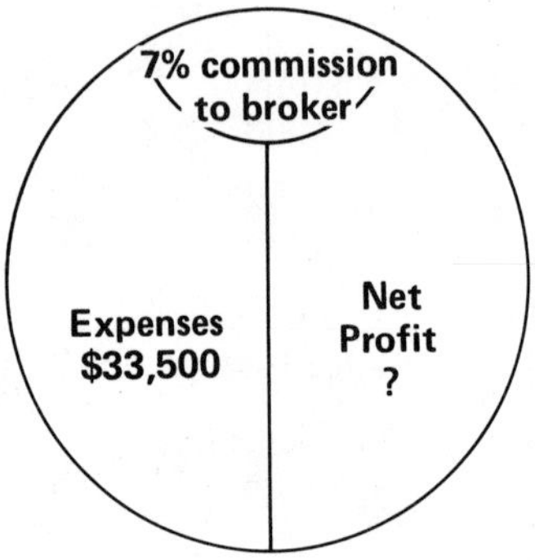

**.93 X $42,000 =
$39,060**

or

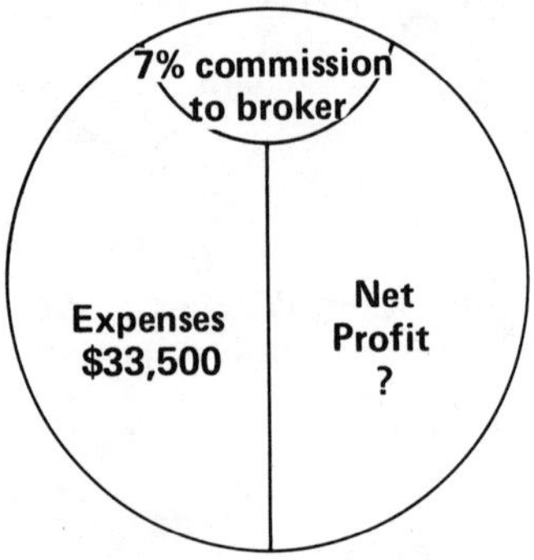

$$\text{Net Profit} = \$39,060 - \$33,500 = \$5560$$

The Net Profit is $5560.

5. In an apartment house, the owner can rent his 8 apartments: (1) $150 per month with utilities, or (2) $120 per month without utilities. If the cost of utilities for 8 apartments costs $800 per year, with which option will the owner's net income be more and by how much?

Solution

We simply take each option separately and then figure out the difference in net income.

Option 1

$$\text{Gross Income} = \$150 \times 8 = \$1200 \text{ per month}$$
$$\$1200 \times 12 = \$14,400 \text{ per year}$$
$$\text{Expenses} = \$800 \text{ (utilities)}$$
$$\text{Net Profit} = ?$$

Using the circle diagram

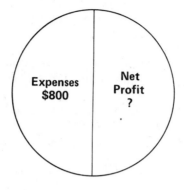

We let this circle represent a gross income of $14,400.

Net Profit in Option 1 = $14,400 − $800 = $13,600

Option 2

Gross Income = $120 × 8 = $960 per month
$960 × 12 = $11,520 per year
Expenses = $0 (theoretically)
Net Profit = ?

Using the circle diagram

We let this circle represent a gross income of $11,520.

Net Profit = $11,520 − $0 = $11,520.

The Net Profit in Option 1 is greater by $13,600 − $11,520 = $2080.

The owner nets $2080 more with Option 1 than with Option 2.

Practice Net Profit Problems

1. If an apartment house owner collected $1000 per year from each of ten tenants and his expenses to maintain the apartment house were $4000, what would be his net profit?

2. A seller netted $16,710.40 from the sale of his home after all expenses. Total costs as shown by settlement statements were $679.60, plus 6 percent commission of the sales price. What did the house sell for?

3. A man bought 5 acres of land for $6000 per acre and divided it into $\frac{1}{4}$-acre lots, which he sold at $2500 per lot. How much did he make on the property?

4. A home lists for $60,000 and sells for 90 percent of the listed price. The original purchase price is $41,000. The owner has spent a total of $8000 on improvements. What is the owner's net profit?

5. A 100-unit apartment house is 20 percent vacant from January to June. The apartments can be rented for: (1) $200 per month with utilities, or (2) $175 per month without utilities. If utilities cost an average of $110 per apartment per year, the net income from January through June would be how much more or less with Option 1?

Solutions to Net Profit Problems

1.

$$\text{Gross Income} = \$1000 \times 10 = \$10,000$$
$$\text{Expenses} = \$4000$$
$$\text{Net Profit} = ?$$

Using the circle diagram

We let this circle represent a gross income of $10,000.

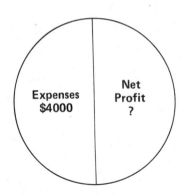

Net Profit = Gross Income − Expenses = $10,000 − $4000 = $6000

The Net Profit is $6000.

2.

94% of Selling Price

or

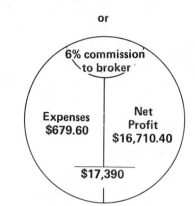

.94 X Selling Price

We add the expenses and net profit together to equal $17,390. Since 94% of the selling price, or .94 X Selling Price = $17,390, we can use the triangle to find the selling price.

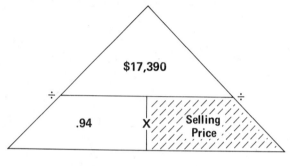

Selling Price = $17,390 ÷ .94 = $18,500

The Selling Price is $18,500.

3. Gross Income = Number of Lots X $2500. Five acres divided into $\frac{1}{4}$-acre lots = 5 ÷ $\frac{1}{4}$ or 5 ÷ .25 lots = 20 lots.

Gross Income = 20 X $2500 = $50,000
Expenses = 5 X $6000 = $30,000
Net Profit = ?

Using the circle diagram

We let this circle represent a gross income of $50,000.

Net Profit = Gross Income − Expenses = $50,000 − $30,000 = $20,000

The Net Profit is $20,000.

Selling Price = 90% of $60,000 = .90 × $60,000 = $54,000
Expenses = $41,000 + $8000 = $49,000
Net Profit = ?

Using the circle diagram

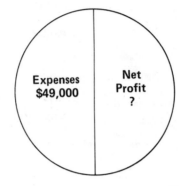

We let this circle represent a
gross income of $54,000.

Net Profit = $54,000 − $49,000 = $5000

The Net Profit is $5000.

5. If a 100-unit apartment house is 20 percent vacant, then only 80 percent of the apartments are occupied, or 80% × 100 or 80 units are occupied.

Option 1

Gross Income = $200 × 80 = $16,000 per month. There are 6 months from January through June. Gross Income = $16,000 × 6 = $96,000 from January through June.
Gross Income = $96,000
Expenses = $110 per apartment per year or $55 per apartment from January through June. There are 80 units occupied; therefore, utilities cost $55 × 80 or $4400 from January through June.

Expenses = $4400
Net Profit = ?

Using the circle diagram

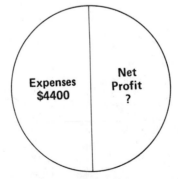

We let this circle represent a
gross income of $96,000.

Net Profit = $96,000 − $4400 = $91,600

The Net Profit with Option 1 is $91,600.

Option 2

Gross Income = $175 × 80 = $14,000 per month. There are 6 months from January through June. Gross Income = $14,000 × 6 = $84,000 from January through June.

$$\text{Gross Income} = \$84,000$$
$$\text{Expenses} = \$0$$
$$\text{Net Profit} = ?$$

Using the circle diagram

We let this circle represent a gross income of $84,000.

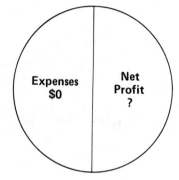

Net Profit = Gross Income − Expenses = $84,000 − $0 = $84,000

The Net Profit with Option 2 = $84,000.

The owner would net $91,600 − $84,000 = $7600 more with Option 1.

8

TAXES

Taxes on any property are arrived at by multiplying the tax rate by the assessed value of the property. The assessed value is often lower than the actual value or appraised value of the property. When the actual value or appraised value is not the same as the assessed value, we find the assessed value by taking a particular percentage (called the tax ratio) of the appraised value. In any one problem, we might be told the assessed value right off, or we might be given the appraised value and the tax ratio and then we must find the assessed value ourselves.

The procedure can best be described by looking at the following example:

Sample Basic Tax Problem

A home that is worth $30,000 is assessed at 80 percent of its actual value. The tax rate is $3.50 per hundred. What are the taxes?

The tax rate must be multiplied by the assessed value to arrive at the tax. Therefore our first job is to find the assessed value. The assessed value is 80 percent of $30,000.

$$80\% \text{ of } \$30,000 =$$
$$.80 \times \$30,000 =$$
$$\$24,000$$

The assessed value is $24,000. The tax rate is $3.50 per $100; that is, for every group of $100, $3.50 in taxes is due. We must now find out how many groups of $100 there are in $24,000. To do this we divide $24,000 by $100.

$$24,000 \div 100 = 240$$

We now have 240 groups of $100, each group being taxed $3.50. We multiply: $240 \times \$3.50 = \$840$.

The taxes are $840.

VARIATION 1

One might be asked to compare taxes using two different tax rates as in the following problems:

What would be the difference in taxes on a $10,000 assessment of property, if the tax rate was $.036 per dollar as compared to $.04 per dollar?

In this particular problem we are given the assessed value right off. We do not have to multiply the appraised value by a tax ratio to arrive at the assessed value.

We can work with each tax rate separately. The first tax rate is $.036 per dollar. That means that every single dollar gets taxed $.036. There are exactly 10,000 one dollar groups in $10,000. Therefore, we simply multiply $.036 \times 10,000 = \$360$.

The second tax rate is $.04 per dollar. Again, each dollar will cost $.04 in taxes. We simply multiply $10,000 \times \$.04 = \$400$ in taxes.

Finding the difference in taxes means subtracting the smaller sum from the larger sum. In this case $400 - $360 = $40 Difference in Taxes.

VARIATION 2

What is the difference in taxes on a $20,000 property if one rate is $3.60 per $100 and the other rate is $.45 per $10? Again, we take each tax rate separately.

The first tax rate is $3.60 per $100. In $20,000 there are $20,000 ÷ $100 or 200 groups of one hundred dollars. The tax rate is $3.60 per hundred. Therefore, 200 × $3.60 = $720 would be the taxes owed.

The second tax rate is $.45 per $10. In $20,000 there are $20,000 ÷ $10 or 2000 groups of ten dollars. The tax rate is $.45 per ten. Therefore, 2000 × $.45 = $900 would be the taxes owed.

The Difference in Taxes is $900 - $720 = $180.

VARIATION 3

A house is valued at $20,000 and assessed at 75 percent of its value. If the tax bill is $600, what is the rate per $100?

$$\text{The Assessed Value} = 75\% \text{ of } \$20,000 = .75 \times \$20,000 = \$15,000$$

Since we are looking for the rate per $100, we can divide $15,000 by $100 to find that there are 150 one hundred dollar groups in $15,000. We know that 150 such groups were multiplied by some tax rate to yield a $600 tax bill. We can use the triangle to find the tax rate.

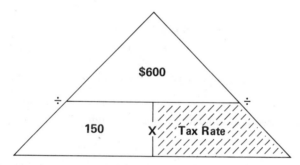

Tax Rate = $600 ÷ 150 = $4 per hundred

Tax Problems with Solutions

1. If a property is assessed at $15,000 and the tax rate is $22 per $1000 of assessed value, how much will you pay in taxes?

Solution

We know the assessed value is $15,000. There are $15,000 ÷ $1000 or 15 groups of one thousand dollars in $15,000.

$$15 \times \$22 = \$330$$

The taxes are $330.

2. If an $8000 lot was assessed at 60 percent of that amount and had a tax rate of $4.21 per $100, what would be the amount of annual taxes?

Solution

$$\text{Assessed Value} = 60\% \text{ of } \$8000 = .60 \times \$8000 = \$4800$$

Rate = \$4.21 per hundred. There are \$4800 ÷ \$100 or 48 groups of one hundred dollars in \$4800. Annual taxes = \$4.21 × 48 = \$202.08.

Annual taxes are \$202.08.

3. If in one community the tax rate is \$2.75 per hundred dollars and in another community it is \$.32 per ten dollars, what is the difference in taxes on two properties assessed for \$42,000 in each community?

Solution

First Community

$$\text{Assessed Value} = \$42,000$$
$$\text{Tax Rate} = \$2.75 \text{ per hundred}$$

There are \$42,000 ÷ 100 or 420 one hundred dollar groups in \$42,000. Since the tax rate is \$2.75 per hundred, the taxes are 420 × \$2.75 or \$1155.

Second Community

$$\text{Assessed Value} = \$42,000$$
$$\text{Tax Rate} = \$.32 \text{ per ten dollars}$$

There are \$42,000 ÷ \$10 or 4200 tens in \$42,000. Since the tax rate is \$.32 per ten dollars, the taxes are \$.32 × 4200 = \$1344.

The Difference in Taxes between Community 1 and Community 2 is \$1344 - \$1155 = \$189 more in Community 2 than in Community 1.

4. If total taxes on a \$12,000 property assessed at 80 percent of its market value is \$393.60, find the rate per \$100.

Solution

$$\text{Assessed Value} = 80\% \text{ of } \$12,000 = .80 \times \$12,000 = \$9600$$

\$9600 ÷ \$100 = 96 groups of \$100
Now, \$393.60 ÷ 96 = \$4.10 per hundred.
The Tax Rate is \$4.10 per hundred.

Practice Tax Problems

1. Taxes on a property are \$646 per year, based on 100 percent valuation, where the tax rate is \$1.90 per \$100 value. What is the assessed value of the property?

2. An $18,000 property is assessed at 75 percent of its value. The tax rate is $7.60 per $100 value. What is the quarterly tax?

3. Find the difference in taxes on a $50,000 property if the tax rate is $.28 per $10 as compared to $.035 per dollar.

Solutions to Tax Problems

1. If the taxes are $646 per year at a tax rate of $1.90 per $100, we divide $646 by $1.90 to find how many groups of $100 there are.

$$\$646 \div \$1.90 = 340$$

There are 340 groups of $100. Therefore, the Assessed Value of the property is $340 \times \$100 = \$34,000$.

The Assessed Value of the property is $34,000.

2. Assessed Value = $75\% \times \$18,000 = .75 \times \$18,000 = \$13,500$

The tax rate is $7.60 per $100. There are $13,500 \div \$100$ or 135 groups of $100 in $13,500.

$$\text{Yearly Tax} = 135 \times \$7.60 = \$1026$$
$$\text{Quarterly Tax} = \$1026 \div 4 = \$256.50$$

The quarterly tax is $256.50.

3. When the tax rate is $.28 per $10, we find how many $10 groups there are in $50,000.

$$\$50,000 \div \$10 = 5000 \text{ groups of ten dollars}$$

Taxes = $5000 \times \$.28 = \$1400$

When the tax rate is $.035 per $1, we use the fact that there are 50,000 $1 groups in $50,000.

Taxes = $50,000 \times \$.035 = \$1750$
The Difference in Taxes is $1750 - 1400 = $350.

9

PRORATION

This type of problem deals with real estate transactions in which expenses such as taxes, water bills, insurance premiums, etc., must be divided between the buyer and the seller when the end of the billing period and the closing date do not coincide.

It is usually the case that the seller has pre-paid one or more bills and sells his home before the end of the billing period. It is then the buyer who owes the seller for the months he would be living "free" of specific bills. Occasionally bills arrive after the sale of the home which should have been paid entirely or in part by the seller of the home. In this case, the buyer ends up paying bills for expenses incurred by the seller before he even occupied the home. The seller would then owe the buyer at closing.

Sample Prorated Problem

A house was sold on November 1, 1977. The seller had pre-paid taxes of $480 for the year January, 1977 through December, 1977. How much does the buyer owe the seller at closing?

First we must figure out how many months of the billing period the buyer and seller lived in the home respectively. (It is important to remember that every month is considered a 30 day month for our purposes.) It is suggested that the old reliable finger-counting method be used to figure out how many months each lived in the home. Although counting on one's fingers doesn't seem very mathematical, it is fool-proof.

The seller lived in the home for the following months of the billing period:

$$\text{January, 1977–October, 1977} = 10 \text{ months}$$

The seller lived in the home for 10 months of the billing period.

The buyer lived in the home for the following months of the billing period:

$$\text{November, 1977–December, 1977} = 2 \text{ months}$$

The buyer lived in the home for 2 months of the billing period.

The total bill is $480 for 12 months. One month's taxes are:

$$\$480 \div 12 = \$40 \text{ per month}$$

Since the seller pre-paid the taxes, the buyer owes the seller 2 months worth of taxes or 2 × $40 = $80.

VARIATION 1

The prorated problem gets slightly more complex when more than one yearly expense has been pre-paid as in the following:

Mr. Buyer took possession of a home bought from Mr. Seller on July 15th. If Mr. Seller paid a water bill of $120 for the year and year's taxes of $720 due on the first of the year, then which of the following is true?

(a) Mr. Buyer owes Mr. Seller $385.

(b) Mr. Seller owes Mr. Buyer $385.
(c) Mr. Buyer owes Mr. Seller $455.
(d) Mr. Seller owes Mr. Buyer $455.

The seller lived in the home for the following months of the billing period:

$$\text{January–June} = 6 \text{ months}$$
$$15 \text{ days in July} = \tfrac{1}{2} \text{ month} = .5 \text{ months}$$

The seller lived in the home for 6.5 months.
The buyer lived in the home for the following months of the billing period:

$$15 \text{ days in July} = \tfrac{1}{2} \text{ month} = .5 \text{ months}$$
$$\text{August–December} = 5 \text{ months}$$

The buyer lived in the home for 5.5 months of the billing period.
Since the seller pre-paid the bills, it is the buyer who owes the seller for 5.5 months worth of expenses.

$$\text{Total Year's Expenses} = \$120 + \$720 = \$840$$
$$\text{Monthly Expenses} = \$840 \div 12 = \$70 \text{ per month}$$

The Buyer owes the Seller 5.5 × $70 = $385 (answer a).

NOTE: In the above problem, if you were pressed for time answers b and d could be eliminated immediately. Certainly it would be the buyer who would owe the money to the seller. Therefore, a or c would be the only possibilities. Eliminating two responses would improve one's chances for guessing if time were of the essence. We call this an educated guess. An educated guess is always better than plain old guessing.

VARIATION 2

Expenses are not always paid on a yearly basis. We might have a prepaid insurance premium that covers a 3 year time period. This would lead us to the following problem:

A 3 year fire insurance policy was purchased on January 1, 1975, by the seller of a home, for $540. If the home was sold on May 10, 1975, how much did the buyer owe the seller of the home? (The insurance premium was paid in January 1975 to cover the 36 months that followed.)

The seller lived in the home for the following months:

$$\text{January 1975–April 1975} = 4 \text{ months}$$
$$10 \text{ days in May 1975} = \tfrac{1}{3} \text{ month} = .33 \text{ month}$$

The seller lived in the home for 4.33 months of the billing period.
The buyer lived in the home for the following months:

$$20 \text{ days in May 1975} = \tfrac{2}{3} \text{ month} = .67 \text{ month}$$
$$\text{June 1975–December 1975} = 7 \text{ months}$$

$$\text{January 1976–December 1976} = 12 \text{ months}$$
$$\text{January 1977–December 1977} = 12 \text{ months}$$

The buyer lived in the home for 31.67 months of the billing period.

Before proceeding any further, we should check that the total billing period is accounted for; that is, between the buyer and the seller the total number of months the home was occupied during the specified billing period was actually 36 months or 3 years.

$$4.33 \text{ months} + 31.67 \text{ months} = 36 \text{ months} = 3 \text{ years}$$

NOTE: It is best to do this step as soon as you can before proceeding only to find you have left out a month or a year somewhere.

The insurance premium was $540 for 36 months or $540 ÷ 36 months = $15 per month. Since the seller pre-paid the policy, the buyer owes the seller 31.67 × $15 = $475.05.

VARIATION 3

Finally, we can be faced with a problem that deals with payments in arrears as in the following:

On December 1st you bought a house. The taxes for the fiscal year, July 1st to June 30th, of $720 have not been paid. Which of the following is true?

(a) You owe the seller $300.
(b) The seller owes you $420.
(c) The seller owes you $300.
(d) You owe the seller $420.

We know that the seller will owe the buyer for taxes which he never paid for the months just prior to his selling the home.

The seller lived in the home for the following months of the billing period:

$$\text{July–November} = 5 \text{ months}$$

You, the buyer, lived in the home for the following months of the billing period:

$$\text{December–June} = 7 \text{ months}$$

Notice that 5 months + 7 months = 12 months. The year's expenses were $720, so the monthly expense was $720 ÷ 12 = $60 per month. The seller owes you 5 × $60 = $300 (answer c).

Prorated Problems with Solutions

1. On January 1st you paid your taxes of $360 for the tax year of January 1st to December 31st. On March 15th you sold your home. What sum of money did the buyer owe you, the seller, for the prorated taxes?

    The seller lived in the home for the following months of the billing period:

    $$\text{January–February} = 2 \text{ months}$$
    $$15 \text{ days in March} = \tfrac{1}{2} \text{ month} = .5 \text{ month}$$

    The seller lived in the home for 2.5 months of the billing period.

    The buyer lived in the home for the following months of the billing period:

$$15 \text{ days in March} = \tfrac{1}{2} \text{ month} = .5 \text{ month}$$
$$\text{April—December} = 9 \text{ months}$$

The buyer lived in the home for 9.5 months of the billing period.

Again we make sure that 2.5 months + 9.5 months = 12 months. Taxes per year = $360. Therefore, taxes per month are $360 ÷ 12 months = $30 per month.

The buyer owed the seller 9.5 × $30 = $285.

2. A fire insurance premium is dated May 1972. It was paid in full for 3 years at a premium of $288. What is the prorated value of the unearned portion as of October 1, 1972?

First we must find how many months are left of the policy from October 1, 1972—April 1975 (the expiration date of the policy).

$$\text{October 1, 1972—April 1973} = 7 \text{ months}$$
$$\text{May 1973—April 1974} = 12 \text{ months}$$
$$\text{May 1974—April 1975} = 12 \text{ months}$$

There are 31 months left on the policy. The total premium is $288 for 36 months. Therefore, the premium is $288 ÷ 36 months = $8 per month. The prorated value of the unearned portion is 31 × $8 = $248.

3. A real estate transaction is closed as of August 10th. The city taxes of $180 and school taxes of $240 have been paid for the year. The yearly county taxes of $126 have not been paid. Compute the proration of taxes between the buyer and the seller. Who owes whom?

In this problem there are some prepaid expenses and some expenses in arrears. We can treat these separately and then even things out at the end.

First we must figure out how long the buyer and seller each occupied the house out of a 12 month period.

The seller lived in the house for the following months of the billing period:

$$\text{January—July} = 7 \text{ months}$$
$$10 \text{ days in August} = \tfrac{1}{3} \text{ month} = .33 \text{ months}$$

The seller lived in the house for a total of 7.33 months of the billing period.

The buyer lived in the house for the following months of the billing period:

$$20 \text{ days in August} = \tfrac{2}{3} \text{ month} = .67 \text{ months}$$
$$\text{September—December} = 4 \text{ months}$$

The buyer lived in the house for a total of 4.67 months of the billing period.

Next we check that 7.33 months + 4.67 months = 12 months.

We take the prepaid expenses first. We add $180 city taxes to $240 school taxes to give us a total of $420 in prepaid expenses. It will be the buyer who will owe the seller 4.67 months worth of prepaid expenses. If the yearly prepaid expenses are $420, the monthly prepaid are $420 ÷ 12 months = $35 per month. The buyer would owe the seller 4.67 × $35 = $163.45.

Looking at the bills in arrears, there are $126 in county taxes for the year. This is $126 ÷ 12 months = $10.50 for the month. The seller would owe the buyer 7.33 × $10.50 = $76.97.

The buyer owes the seller $163.45. The seller owes the buyer $76.97. The difference between these is $86.48. This amount is to be paid by the buyer to the seller.

4. Taxes for the fiscal year January 1st to December 30th had not been paid when a home was sold on April 15th. If the year's taxes are $756, what does the seller owe the buyer at the closing?

The seller lived in the house for the following months of the billing period:

$$January-March = 3 \text{ months}$$
$$15 \text{ days in April} = \tfrac{1}{2} \text{ month} = .5 \text{ month}$$

The seller lived in the house for 3.5 months of the billing period.

The buyer lived in the house for the following months of the billing period:

$$15 \text{ days in April} = \tfrac{1}{2} \text{ month} = .5 \text{ month}$$
$$May-December = 8 \text{ months}$$

The buyer lived in the house for 8.5 months of the billing period.

First we check to see that 3.5 months + 8.5 months = 12 months.

If the yearly taxes are $756, the month's taxes will be $756 ÷ 12 months = $63 per month.

Since the buyer will be paying for the 3.5 months that he didn't occupy the home, the seller will owe the buyer 3.5 × $63 = $220.50.

Practice Prorated Problems

1. A house is sold on June 1st. The taxes of $480 for the calendar year have been paid, as well as a fire insurance premium of $84 for the year. What does the buyer owe the seller at closing?

2. On January 1, 1974, a three year fire insurance policy for $216 was purchased. Taxes for the year of 1974 of $672 were paid. The house was sold on September 15, 1974. What does the buyer owe the seller at closing?

3. Mr. Halpern sold his home on March 1, 1976. Taxes of $762 for the 1976 fiscal year January to December were not paid by the time of closing. Mr. Smith, the buyer of the home, would have to pay the full year's taxes. How much did Mr. Halpern owe Mr. Smith?

Solutions to Prorated Problems

1. The seller lived in the house for the following months of the billing period:

$$January-May = 5 \text{ months}$$

The seller lived in the house for 5 months out of the billing period.

The buyer lived in the house for the following months of the billing period:

$$June-December = 7 \text{ months}$$

The buyer lived in the house for 7 months of the billing period.

The year's pre-paid expenses are $480 + $84 = $564. The monthly expenses are $564 ÷ 12 = $47.

The buyer owes the seller 7 months worth of expenses or 7 X $47 = $329.

The buyer owes the seller $329.

2. Since the fire insurance covers a 3 year period and the taxes cover a yearly period, it would be easiest to deal with these separately.

Fire Insurance Premium

The seller lived in the house for the following months of the billing period:

$$\text{January 1974—August 1974} = 8 \text{ months}$$
$$15 \text{ days in September } 1974 = \tfrac{1}{2} \text{ month} = .5 \text{ month}$$

The seller lived in the house for a total of 8.5 months of the billing period.

The buyer lived in the house for the following months of the billing period:

$$15 \text{ days in September } 1974 = \tfrac{1}{2} \text{ month} = .5 \text{ month}$$
$$\text{October 1974—December 1974} = 3 \text{ months}$$
$$\text{January 1975—December 1975} = 12 \text{ months}$$
$$\text{January 1976—December 1976} = 12 \text{ months}$$

The buyer lived in the house for a total of 27.5 months of the billing period.

The fire insurance premium was $216 for 36 months or $216 ÷ 36 months = $6 per month. The buyer owed the seller for 27.5 months worth of premiums = 27.5 X $6 = $165.

Taxes

The seller lived in the house for the following months of the billing period:

$$\text{January 1974—August 1974} = 8 \text{ months}$$
$$15 \text{ days in September} = \tfrac{1}{2} \text{ month} = .5 \text{ month}$$

The seller lived in the house for a total of 8.5 months of the billing period.

The buyer lived in the house for the following months of the billing period:

$$15 \text{ days in September} = \tfrac{1}{2} \text{ month} = .5 \text{ month}$$
$$\text{October 1974—December 1974} = 3 \text{ months}$$

The buyer lived in the house for a total of 3.5 months of the billing period.

The taxes were $672 for the year or $672 ÷ 12 months = $56 per month. The buyer owes the seller for 3.5 months worth of expenses or 3.5 X $56 = $196.

In summary, the buyer owes the seller $165 for fire insurance premiums plus $196 for taxes for a total of $361.

The buyer owes the seller $361.

3. The seller lived in the house for the following months of the billing period:

$$\text{January—February} = 2 \text{ months}$$

The seller lived in the home for 2 months of the billing period.

The buyer lived in the home for the following months of the billing period:

$$\text{March—December} = 10 \text{ months}$$

The buyer lived in the home for 10 months of the billing period.

The taxes for the year are $762. Taxes for the month are $762 ÷ 12 = $63.50.

Since it is the buyer who will have to pay the whole year's taxes, the seller will owe the buyer 2 months worth of taxes or 2 X $63.50 = $127.

Mr. Halpern owes Mr. Smith $127.

10

MEASUREMENT

A prerequisite for dealing with measurement problems is to know the basic relationships between our units of measure. A list to be memorized is below:

12 inches = 1 foot
3 feet = 1 yard
5280 feet = 1 mile
1 square yard = 9 square feet
1 cubic yard = 27 cubic feet
1 acre = 43,560 square feet = 4840 square yards

Measurement problems make it necessary to add, subtract, multiply and divide various units of measure. We cannot perform these basic operations unless we are working with the same units of measure at all times. For example, we cannot add feet and yards or subtract inches and feet. We sometimes must convert one unit of measure to another unit of measure.

When converting a larger unit of measure to a smaller unit of measure, we are working with smaller "pieces" and, therefore, more of them. We will have to multiply. For example, to change 6 yards to feet, we would multiply 6 X 3 = 18 feet. How many inches in 4 yards? First, change 4 yards to 4 X 3 feet or 12 feet; 12 feet is changed to 12 X 12 inches or 144 inches. Four yards = 144 inches.

14 yards = _____ feet
6 feet = _____ inches
2 cubic yards = _____ cubic feet

When converting a smaller unit of measure into a larger unit of measure we divide, since the bigger the "pieces," the fewer we would have. For example, to change 48 inches to feet, we divide 48 by 12 and get 4 feet.

96 inches = _____ feet
21 feet = _____ yards
54 cubic feet = _____ cubic yards

AREA

The area of any surface is the number of 1 X 1 unit squares which will fit on that surface. Area is always measured in square units. It is important to make sure that we are working with like units of measure.

Rectangles

A rectangle is a four-sided figure with 4 right angles, in which both pairs of opposite sides are equal and parallel (right angles = 90°).

93

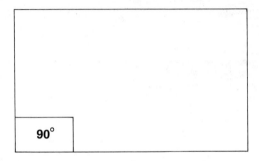

Area of a Rectangle = Length × Width

For example: The length of a rectangular-shaped room is 15 ft. and the width is 10 ft. Find the area.

The Area = Length × Width = 15 ft. × 10 ft. = 150 square ft.

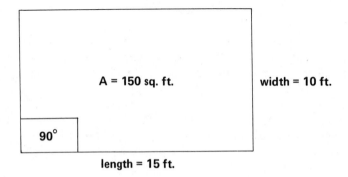

Suppose we were given a rectangle whose length = 4 yds. and whose width = 10 ft.

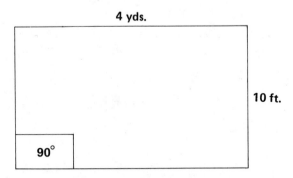

It would be tempting at first to multiply 10 × 4 = 40. Notice we don't know 40 square "whats." We have the length in yards and the width in feet. We first have to convert yards to feet or feet to yards. We know 4 yards = 4 × 3 feet = 12 feet. Now, length = 12 feet and width = 10 feet.

Area = Length × Width = 12 × 10 = 120 square ft.

Squares

A square is a special rectangle in which the length and the width are equal. Look at the following square.

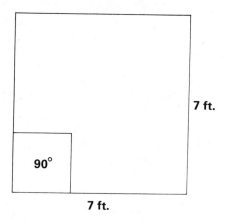

Length = 7 ft. and Width = 7 ft.
Area = 7 X 7 = 49 square ft.

Triangles

There are two formulas for triangles, one for a general triangle and the other for a right triangle. It is the right triangle which is used more often on the Real Estate Exam. Both formulas are discussed below.

General Triangles

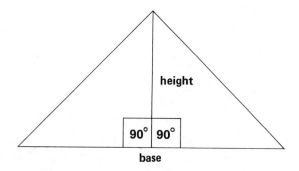

Any side of a triangle is called the base. A line drawn to that side from the opposite corner at a right angle is called the height. The formula for area of a triangle is as follows:

$$\text{Area} = \frac{\text{Base} \times \text{Height}}{2}$$

Consider the following triangle

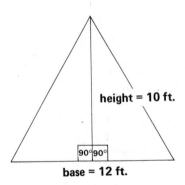

$$\text{Area} = \frac{\text{Base} \times \text{Height}}{2}$$

$$\frac{12 \times 10}{2} = \frac{120}{2} = 60 \text{ square ft.}$$

Right Triangles

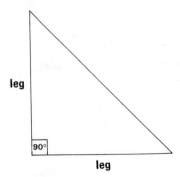

    A right triangle is special since two of the sides meet at a right angle. These sides are called the legs of the triangle. The third side, the longest diagonal side, is **NOT NEEDED** to find the area of a right triangle. This is very important to remember, since we are sometimes told the length of this side in addition to the length of the legs. It is human nature to want to use every number given in a math problem. The area of a right triangle is as follows:

$$\text{Area} = \frac{\text{Leg} \times \text{Leg}}{2}$$

Consider the following.

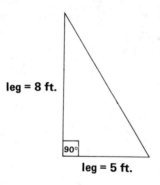

$$\text{Area} = \frac{\text{Leg} \times \text{Leg}}{2} = \frac{8 \text{ ft.} \times 5 \text{ ft.}}{2} = \frac{40 \text{ sq. ft.}}{2} = 20 \text{ square ft.}$$

Once again, we must make sure we are using just one unit of measure when we are computing our answer. For example

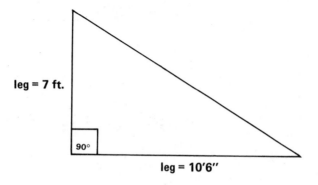

Before using the formula to find the area of the triangle above, we must change 10 ft. 6 in. to something more workable. Since 6 in. = $\frac{1}{2}$ ft., 10 ft. 6 in. = $10\frac{1}{2}$ ft. = 10.5 ft. Now we can proceed.

$$\text{Area} = \frac{\text{Leg} \times \text{Leg}}{2} = \frac{10.5 \times 7}{2} = \frac{73.50}{2} = 36.75 \text{ square ft.}$$

Trapezoids

A trapezoid is a four-sided figure in which two sides are parallel and two sides are not parallel. The following are all trapezoids.

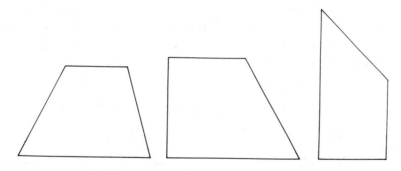

There are two ways to find the area of a trapezoid. In the first way, we can simply break the trapezoid into rectangles and triangles, find those areas, and sum them up. The other method is to use the specific trapezoid formula. Using the following diagram, both methods are illustrated.

Find the area of this trapezoid.

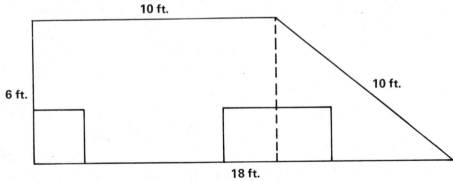

 Method 1

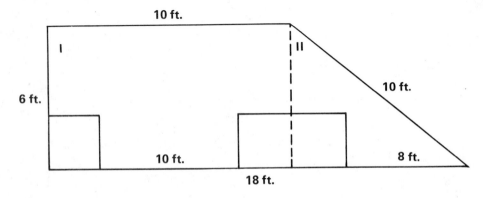

Figure 1 is a rectangle.

$$\text{Area Figure 1} = \text{Length} \times \text{Width} = 10 \times 6 = 60 \text{ square ft.}$$

Figure 2 is a right triangle. To find the area we have to know the length of both legs. The legs are 6 ft. and 8 ft. Notice, we do not use the diagonal side of the right triangle to find the area.

$$\text{Area figure 2} = \frac{\text{Leg} \times \text{Leg}}{2} = \frac{8 \times 6}{2} = \frac{48}{2} = 24 \text{ square ft.}$$

Area figure 1 + Area figure 2 = 60 sq. ft. + 24 sq. ft. = 84 square ft.

 Method 2

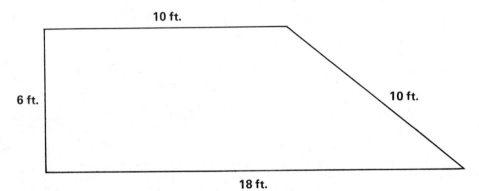

The parallel sides of the trapezoid are called the bases. The shortest (straight) distance between them is called the height. The following formula is the specific formula for the area of a trapezoid:

$$\text{Area} = \frac{(\text{Base} + \text{Base}) \times \text{Height}}{2}$$

In the trapezoid being discussed, the bases are 18 ft. and 10 ft., and the height is 6 ft. Again, notice we do not use the diagonal 10 ft. side.

$$\text{Area} = \frac{(18 + 10) \times 6}{2} = \frac{28 \times 6}{2} = \frac{168}{2} = 84 \text{ square ft.}$$

Either method for finding the area of a trapezoid can be used. One method could be used to check the other method. Use the one with which you feel more comfortable.

PERIMETER

To find the perimeter of any geometric shape, we simply find the distance around that shape. For example, the perimeter of the following rectangle 8 in. long and 5 in. wide would be 8 in. + 5 in. + 8 in. + 5 in. = 26 in.

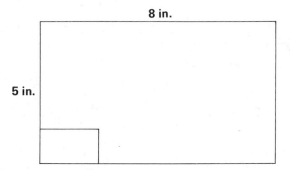

VOLUME

The volume of a space is the capacity of the space; that is, how many $1 \times 1 \times 1$-unit cubes the space could hold. To measure volume we use three dimensions. You need only to familiarize yourself with the volume of a rectangular shape figure.

$$\text{Volume} = \text{Length} \times \text{Width} \times \text{Height}$$

The answer will of course be in cubic inches, feet, yards, etc.

If a room is 10 ft. long, 7 ft. wide, and 8 ft. high, find the volume.

$$\text{Volume} = 10 \times 7 \times 8 = 560 \text{ cubic ft.}$$

COMPARING MEASUREMENTS

We can compare two measurements by using a fraction. As in Chapter 1, which dealt with fractions, when we compare two numbers the number we are comparing *to* always goes in the denominator of the fraction (bottom part of the fraction). The number we are holding up for comparison goes in the numerator (top part of the fraction). Two numbers can be compared by using a fraction or we can go one step further and change the fraction to a decimal and then to a percent. Consider the following

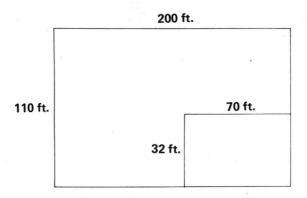

200 ft.

110 ft.   70 ft.

32 ft.

Looking at the above diagram, which fraction best describes the area of the smaller rectangle compared to the area of the larger rectangle?

(a) $\frac{1}{8}$

(b) $\frac{2}{3}$

(c) $\frac{1}{2}$

(d) $\frac{1}{10}$

Our first step is to find the areas of both rectangles.

Area large rectangle = Length × Width = 200 ft. × 110 ft. = 22,000 square ft.
Area small rectangle = Length × Width = 70 ft. × 32 ft. = 2240 square ft.

To compare the area of the smaller rectangle to the area of the larger rectangle, we place the area of the smaller in the numerator of the fraction and the area of the larger in the denominator of the fraction. The fraction looks like this

$$\frac{2240 \text{ sq. ft.}}{22,000 \text{ sq. ft.}} = \frac{2240}{22,000}$$

If we were to round off 2240 to 2200, the fraction would become

$$\frac{2200}{22,000} = \frac{1}{10} \quad \text{(answer d)}$$

If we had been asked to find what percent the smaller rectangle is of the larger rectangle, we would change the fraction $\frac{1}{10}$ to .10 (by dividing the numerator by the denominator) and then change .10 to 10%.

Sometimes we are required to find the area of shaded portions of diagrams. For example, find the shaded portion of the following.

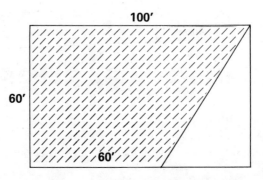

100′

60′

60′

Method 1

The shaded figure can be divided into a rectangle and a right triangle as shown below.

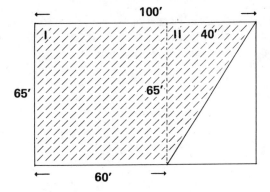

Figure 1 is a rectangle and figure 2 is a right triangle.

$$\text{Area 1} = \text{Length} \times \text{Width} = 65 \text{ ft.} \times 60 \text{ ft.} = 3900 \text{ square ft.}$$

$$\text{Area 2} = \frac{\text{Leg} \times \text{Leg}}{2} = \frac{65 \times 40}{2} = \frac{2600}{2} = 1300 \text{ square ft.}$$

Area figure 1 + figure 2 = 3900 sq. ft. + 1300 sq. ft. = 5200 square ft.

Method 2

The area of the shaded portion above could be found by using the formula for the area of a trapezoid. (The figure is a trapezoid since it has 4 sides, two parallel and two not parallel.) The bases are 100 ft. and 60 ft. and the height is 65 ft.

$$\text{Area} = \frac{(\text{Base} + \text{Base}) \times \text{Height}}{2} =$$

$$\frac{(100 + 60) \times 65}{2} =$$

$$\frac{160 \times 65}{2} =$$

$$\frac{10,400}{2} =$$

$$5200 \text{ sq. ft.}$$

Notice the answers using method 1 and method 2 are the same. It does not matter which method is used.

MEASUREMENT AND MONEY

It is not uncommon to deal with measurement problems that involve dollars and cents as well. For example: A lot costs $2.00 per square foot. The dimensions are 100 ft. × 75 ft. Find the total cost.

First, we must find the area of the lot in square feet. We know the formula for the area of a rectangle is:

$$\text{Area} = \text{Length} \times \text{Width} = 100 \text{ ft.} \times 75 \text{ ft.} = 7500 \text{ square ft.}$$

Since we have 7500 sq. ft. at $2.00 per sq. ft., the total cost will be 7500 × $2.00 = $15,000.

THE METRIC SYSTEM

Many countries in the world presently use the metric system as a system of measurement. There is good reason to believe that the United States will follow suit in the near future. Many states have already incorporated the metric system into the Real Estate Exams and it is likely that more states will be doing the same.

The meter is the basic metric unit for length. Various prefixes are used to express parts of one meter or multiples of the meter.

Metric Conversion Table

1 millimeter (mm) = 1/1000 of a meter = .001 meter
1 centimeter (cm) = 1/100 of a meter = .01 meter
1 decimeter (dm) = 1/10 of a meter = .1 meter
1 dekameter (dkm) = 10 meters
1 hectometer (hm) = 100 meters
1 kilometer (km) = 1000 meters

Metric Units and U.S. Equivalents

1 meter = 39.37 inches
1 mm = .04 inches
1 cm = .39 inches
1 km = .62 miles
2.54 cm = 1 inch
.3 m = 1 foot
.91 m = 1 yard
1.61 km = 1 mile

Measurement Problems with Solutions

1.   Find the area of the following.

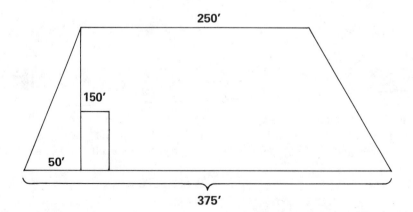

Solution

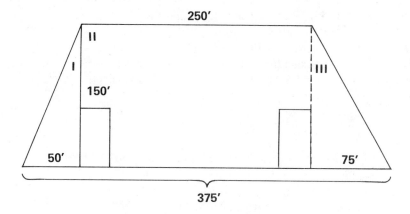

Method 1

(A dotted line represents any line that has been drawn into the problem to help solve it.)

$$\text{Area (triangle) } 1 = \frac{\text{Leg} \times \text{Leg}}{2} = \frac{50 \text{ ft.} \times 150 \text{ ft.}}{2} = \frac{7500}{2} = 3750 \text{ square ft.}$$

$$\text{Area (rectangle) } 2 = \text{Length} \times \text{Width} = 250 \text{ ft.} \times 150 \text{ ft.} = 37{,}500 \text{ square ft.}$$

$$\text{Area (triangle) } 3 = \frac{\text{Leg} \times \text{Leg}}{2} = \frac{75 \text{ ft.} \times 150 \text{ ft.}}{2} = \frac{11{,}250}{2} = 5625 \text{ square ft.}$$

Area 1 + 2 + 3 = 3750 + 37,500 + 5625 = 46,875 square ft.

Method 2

$$\text{Area trapezoid} = \frac{(\text{Base} + \text{Base}) \times \text{Height}}{2} =$$

$$\frac{(375 + 250) \times 150}{2} =$$

$$\frac{625 \times 150}{2} = \frac{93{,}750}{2} =$$

46,875 square ft.

The area of the figure is 46,875 square feet.

2. How many acres is the area of a lot 300 ft. by 450 ft.?

Solution

First, we find how many square feet there are in the lot.

$$\text{Area} = \text{Length} \times \text{Width} = 450 \text{ ft.} \times 300 \text{ ft.} = 135{,}000 \text{ square ft.}$$

We want to convert square feet to acres. We are changing a smaller unit of measure, square feet, to a larger unit of measure, acres. Therefore, we use division. We divide 135,000 square feet by 43,560 (1 acre = 43,650 square feet.) giving us 3.10 acres, which is approximately 3 acres.

3. A building is 75 ft. long, 25 ft. deep, and 36 ft. high.
 (a) How many cubic feet are there in the building?
 (b) What would be the value of the building if it were worth $3.50 per cubic foot?

Solution

(a) Volume = Length × Width × Height = 75 ft. × 25 ft. × 36 ft. = 67,500 cubic ft.
(b) At $3.50 per cubic foot, the value would be:

$$67,500 \times \$3.50 = \$236,250$$

There are 67,500 cubic feet in the building, valued at $236,250.

4. What portion of the following rectangle has been removed from the upper right hand corner?

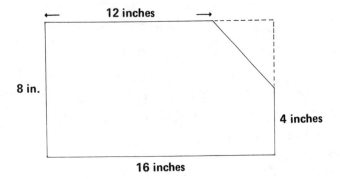

Solution

We want to compare the area of the triangle which has been removed with the area of the original rectangle.

$$\text{Area triangle} = \frac{\text{Leg} \times \text{Leg}}{2} = \frac{4 \text{ in.} \times 4 \text{ in.}}{2} = \frac{16 \text{ sq. in.}}{2} = 8 \text{ square in.}$$

Area original rectangle = Length × Width = 16 in. × 8 in. = 128 square in.

A fraction can be used to compare two numbers. The number we are holding up for comparison is the area of the triangle. Therefore, it belongs in the numerator of the fraction. The number we are comparing to is the area of the rectangle. Therefore, it belongs in the denominator of the fraction.

$$\frac{8 \text{ sq. in.}}{128 \text{ sq. in.}} = \frac{1}{16}$$

$\frac{1}{16}$ of the rectangle has been removed.

5. What is the perimeter of a lot 50 ft. × 100 ft.?

Solution

It is a good idea to sketch the lot first.

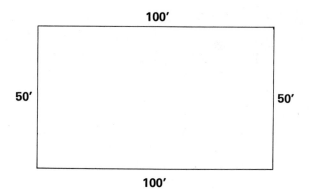

The perimeter is simply the sum of the sides.

$$\text{Perimeter} = 100 \text{ ft.} + 50 \text{ ft.} + 100 \text{ ft.} + 50 \text{ ft.} = 300 \text{ ft.}$$

The perimeter is 300 feet.

Practice Measurement Problems

1. Find the area of the shaded portion shown below.

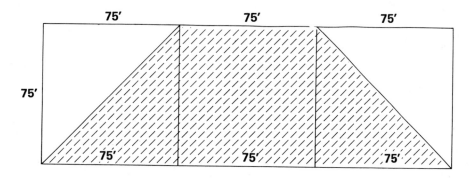

2. A basement 20 ft. by 30 ft. by 5 ft. would contain how many cubic yds.?

3. Write the formula for the area of a rectangle, triangle, right triangle, and trapezoid.

4. (a) 4 ft. = _____ in.
    (b) 48 ft. = _____ yds.
    (c) 216 in. = _____ yds.
    (d) 4,356,000 sq. ft. = _____ acres
    (e) 81 cubic ft. = _____ cubic yds.

5. You sell a lot that measures 75 ft. frontage on the street and 150 ft. 8 in. in depth. How many square ft. in the lot?

6. A rectangular piece of ground has a frontage of 300 ft. and a depth of 726 ft. At $750 per acre, what is the selling price?

Solutions to Measurement Problems

1.

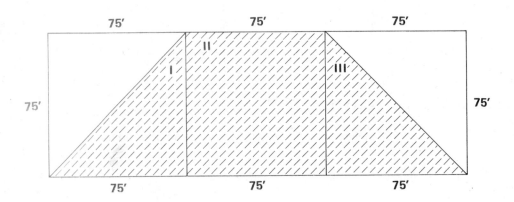

Method 1

$$\text{Area (triangle) 1} = \frac{\text{Leg} \times \text{Leg}}{2} = \frac{75 \text{ ft.} \times 75 \text{ ft.}}{2} = \frac{5625}{2} = 2812.5 \text{ square ft.}$$

$$\text{Area (rectangle) 2} = \text{Length} \times \text{Width} = 75 \text{ ft.} \times 75 \text{ ft.} = 5625 \text{ square ft.}$$

$$\text{Area (triangle) 3} = \frac{\text{Leg} \times \text{Leg}}{2} = \frac{75 \text{ ft.} \times 75 \text{ ft.}}{2} = \frac{5625}{2} = 2812.5 \text{ square ft.}$$

Area 1 + 2 + 3 = 2812.5 + 5625 + 2812.5 = 11,250 square ft.
The area of the shaded portion is 11,250 square feet.

Method 2

The shaded portion is a trapezoid.

$$\text{Area trapezoid} = \frac{(\text{Base} + \text{Base}) \times \text{Height}}{2} =$$

$$\frac{(225 \text{ ft.} + 75 \text{ ft.}) \times 75 \text{ ft.}}{} =$$

$$\frac{300 \text{ ft.} \times 75 \text{ ft.}}{2} =$$

$$\frac{22,500 \text{ sq. ft.}}{2} =$$

11,250 square ft.

2. Volume = Length × Width × Height = 20 ft. × 30 ft. × 5 ft. = 600 × 5 = 3000 cubic ft.
    1 cubic yd. = 27 cubic ft. Since we are going from a smaller unit of measure to a larger unit of measure, we must divide by 27.

$$3000 \text{ cubic ft.} \div 27 = 111.11 \text{ cubic yds.}$$

3. Area rectangle = Length × Width
    $$\text{Area triangle} = \frac{\text{Base} \times \text{Height}}{2}$$
    $$\text{Area right triangle} = \frac{\text{Leg} \times \text{Leg}}{2}$$
    $$\text{Area trapezoid} = \frac{(\text{Base} + \text{Base}) \times \text{Height}}{2}$$

4. (a) 4 ft. = 4 × 12 = 48 in.
    (b) 48 ft. = 48 ÷ 3 = 16 yds.
    (c) 216 in. = 216 ÷ 12 = 18 ft.; 18 ft. ÷ 3 = 6 yds.
    (d) 4,356,000 sq. ft. = 4,356,000 ÷ 43,560 acres = 100 acres
    (e) 81 cubic ft. = 81 ÷ 27 cubic yds. = 3 cubic yards.

5. 150 ft. 8 in. = $150\frac{2}{3}$ ft. (8 in. = $\frac{2}{3}$ ft.) = 150.67 ft.
    Area = Length × Width = 150.67 ft. × 75 ft. = 11,300.25 square ft.

6. To find the number of acres, we find the number of square feet in the property.

$$\text{Area} = \text{Length} \times \text{Width} = 300 \text{ ft.} \times 726 \text{ ft.} = 217,800 \text{ square ft.}$$

To find how many acres in the lot, divide the number of square feet by 43,560.

$$217,800 \div 43,560 = 5$$

There are 5 acres. Each costs $750. The selling price is $750 × 5 = $3750.

11

JUST FOR BROKERS

Although the basic skills needed for the broker's and salesman's exams are similar in many ways, there is a difference in emphasis placed on various topics. In particular, capitalization, net profit, and measurement are of great importance to those taking the broker's exam.

In this chapter, we will deal with capitalization for the first time and discuss more variations of net profit and measurement, both of which have already been presented. In addition, the concept of percents is more crucial to the broker's exam and therefore a brief review of percents will be presented. Of course, all other topics dealt with in previous chapters are required for the broker as well as the salesman.

Capitalization

The basic formula for capitalization problems is as follows:

Value $\times$ Rate of Capitalization = Net Income

In the formula above it is important to remember that the net profit is the sum of money left after expenses have been subtracted from the gross income.

Once again, we can use the triangle method, setting it up as follows

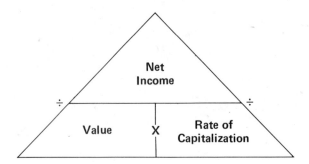

Sample Basic Capitalization Problems

An investor nets $20,000 per year which represents a 10 percent rate of capitalization. What is the value of his property?

Value = ?
Rate of Capitalization = 10% = .10
Net Income = $20,000

Using the triangle

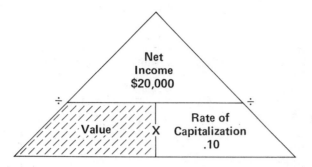

Value = $20,000 ÷ .10 = $200,000.

VARIATION 1

Frequently, rather than being given the net profit right off, we are given the gross income and expenses, which will enable us to arrive at the net profit we need. For example:

If an investor desires a return of 8 percent, what is the maximum price he can offer to pay for a rental property if the rental income is $8000 per year with expenses totalling $2400 per annum? (The price he pays will be the value of the property.)

Value = ?

Rate of Capitalization = 8% = .08

Net Income = Gross Income - Expenses = $8000 - 2400 = $5600

Using the triangle

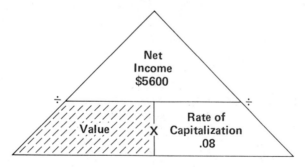

Value = $5600 ÷ .08 = $70,000.

VARIATION 2

We have a slightly different problem when we are told the net income is a percent of the gross income. For example:

The annual gross income on a property is $50,000. The net income is 55 percent of the gross income. If the rate of net return is 12 percent, what is the value of the property?

Value = ?

Rate of Net Return = 12% (Rate of Net Return = Rate of Capitalization)

Net Income = 55% of Gross Income = .55 × $50,000 = $27,500

Now using the triangle

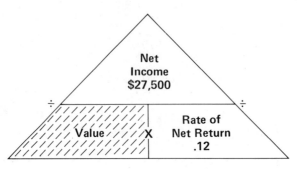

Value = $27,500 ÷ .12 = $229,166.67.

VARIATION 3

Finally, we are sometimes faced with the following situation:

An investment property has a net capitalized value of $100,000. If the expenses are 55 percent of the gross income and the rate of capitalization is 10 percent, find the gross income.

Our formula has three unknowns: value, rate of capitalization, and net income. We know enough information to find our net income. Once we know the net income we will be able to use the remaining information for finding the gross income.

$$Value = \$100,000$$
$$Rate\ of\ Capitalization = 10\% = .10$$
$$Net\ Income = ?$$

Using the triangle

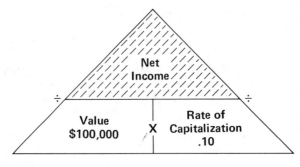

Net Income = $100,000 × .10 = $10,000.

We now know that the net income is $10,000. If expenses are 55 percent of the gross income, then the net income would be 45 percent of the gross income. We now have the following equation:

$$\$10,000 = 45\%\ of\ Gross\ Income$$
$$or$$
$$\$10,000 = .45 \times Gross\ Income$$

We can use the triangle method to help us find the gross income.

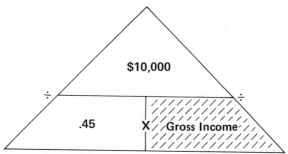

Gross Income = $10,000 ÷ .45 = $22,222.22.

Additional Net Profit Problems with Solutions

1. A seller would like to net $3000 plus equity of $10,000 upon selling his property. He has a mortgage balance of $12,000. The broker's fee is 6 percent. What is the minimum selling price?

Solution

If the equity is $10,000 and the mortgage balance is $12,000, the purchase price was $22,000. Therefore, expenses were $22,000. Using the circle diagram

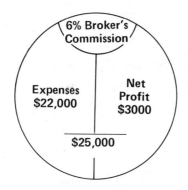

94% of the Selling Price = $25,000

or

.94 × Selling Price = $25,000

Putting this information into the triangle

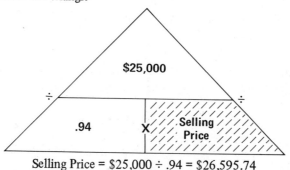

Selling Price = $25,000 ÷ .94 = $26,595.74

The minimum selling price is $26,595.74.

2.   Mr. Plan bought land for $45,000. He built 20 homes on the lots and incurred additional expenses of $500,000. If the net profit represents 12 percent of the gross income, what must be the selling price of each home?

Solution

If the net profit represents 12 percent of the gross, the expenses must represent the difference or 88 percent of the gross. Expenses are $45,000 + $500,000 or $545,000. Therefore

$$\text{Expenses} = 88\% \text{ of Gross}$$
or
$$\$545,000 = .88 \times \text{Gross}$$

Using the triangle

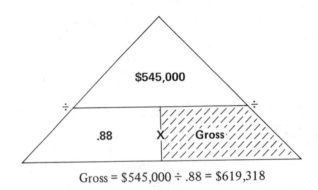

$$\text{Gross} = \$545,000 \div .88 = \$619,318$$

If 20 homes sell for $619,318, then 1 home sells for $619,318 ÷ 20 or $30,866.

3.   An apartment house owner has 10 apartments renting for $225 per month. He paid a manager 5 percent of gross income. Other expenses average $2000 per year. Find the net average monthly income.

Solution

$$\text{Gross Income} = 10 \times \$225 \text{ (per month)} = \$2250 \text{ per month}$$
$$= \$2250 \times 12 \text{ (per year)} = \$27,000 \text{ per year}$$

The manager gets 5% of $27,000 = .05 × $27,000 = $1350.
Total Expenses = $2000 + 1350 = $3350.
Using the circle diagram

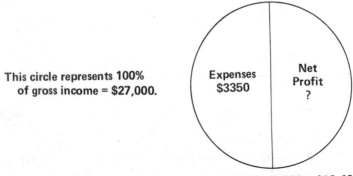

This circle represents 100% of gross income = $27,000.

Expenses $3350

Net Profit ?

$$\text{Net Income} = \$27,000 - \$3350 = \$23,650 \text{ per year}$$

Net Income per month = $23,650 ÷ 12 = $1970.83.

Additional Measurement Problems with Solutions

1. Find the area of the following plot in acres

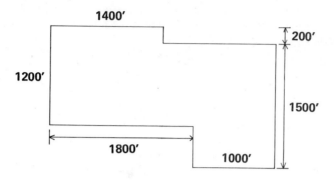

Solution

The plot must be divided into rectangles whose areas we can compute and sum.

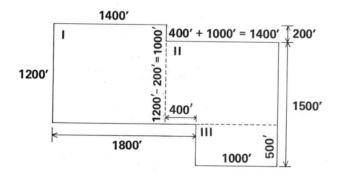

Area I = Length × Width = 1400 ft. × 1200 ft. = 1,680,000 square ft.
Area II = Length × Width = 1400 ft. × 1000 ft. = 1,400,000 square ft.
Area III = Length × Width = 1000 ft. × 500 ft. = 500,000 square ft.

Area I + II + III = 3,580,000 square ft.

To convert square feet to acres we are going from a smaller unit of measure to a larger unit of measure and therefore we divide. We know that 43,560 sq. ft. = 1 acre. Then, 3,580,000 ÷ 43,560 = 82 acres (approximately).

2. If a house is 80 ft. × 100 ft. and sells for $24,000, find the reproduction cost of the house per square foot.

Solution

We find the area of the house in the following way:

$$\text{Area} = \text{Length} \times \text{Width} = 80 \text{ ft.} \times 100 \text{ ft.} = 8000 \text{ square ft.}$$

To find the cost per square foot, we divide the total price by the number of square feet:

$$\$24,000 \div 8000 \text{ sq. ft.} = \$3 \text{ per sq. ft.}$$

The reproduction cost is $3 per square foot.

3. Find the total cost of the house and lot pictured below if the house costs $15 per square foot and the lot costs $1 per square foot.

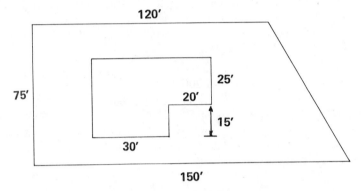

Solution

We can work on each of these separately:

(a) The lot is a trapezoid.

$$\text{Area of a trapezoid} = \frac{(\text{Base} + \text{Base}) \times \text{Height}}{2} =$$

$$\frac{(120 \text{ ft.} + 150 \text{ ft.}) \times 75}{2} =$$

$$10,125 \text{ square ft.}$$

The lot costs $1 per square foot.

$$10,125 \times \$1 = \$10,125.$$

(b) The area of the house can be found by breaking the diagram into two rectangles as follows.

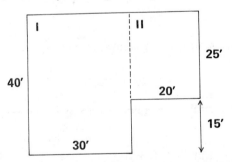

Area I = Length × Width = 40 ft. × 30 ft. = 1200 square ft.
Area II = Length × Width = 20 ft. × 25 ft. = 500 square ft.

Area I + II = 1200 sq. ft. + 500 sq. ft. = 1700 square ft.
The house costs $15 per square foot.

$$1700 \times \$15 = \$25,500$$

The total cost of the house and the lot = $25,500 + $10,125 = $35,625.

Review of Percents

To find a percent of a number, we must first change the percent to a decimal and then multiply the decimal by the number:

$$18\% \text{ of } 200 = .18 \times 200 = 36$$

To find what percent one number is of another number, we first indicate the relationship as a fraction. The number we are holding up for comparison goes in the numerator of the fraction while the number we are comparing to goes in the denominator of the fraction. We may then change the fraction to a decimal and then to a percent. For example, 20 is what percent of 80?

$$\frac{20}{80} = .25 = 25\%$$

This concept of finding what percent one number is of another number can be mixed in with basic measurement problems as in the following examples:

1. A builder wants to divide the property shown below into five lots and build a 1500-square foot home on each lot. Four of the lots will have 100-foot frontage and both sides of the lot lines will be perpendicular to the street. The fifth house will occupy what percent of the lot area?

600'

100'

500'

Solution

First we must find the area of the fifth lot. The fifth lot is a trapezoid.

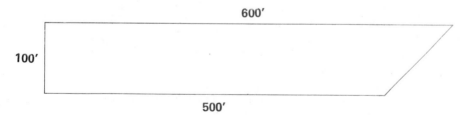

$$\text{Area of a trapezoid} = \frac{(\text{Base} + \text{Base}) \times \text{Height}}{2} =$$

$$\frac{(200 + 100) \times 100}{2} =$$

$$15,000 \text{ square ft.}$$

To find what percent the house is of the lot we write the fraction:

$$\frac{1500 \text{ sq. ft.}}{15,000 \text{ sq. ft.}} = .10 = 10\%$$

The fifth house is 10% of the lot area.

A slightly more complicated problem with measurement and percent follows.

2. The house shown below is parallel to the street and costs $30 per square foot. The owner wants to add a garage twenty-five feet wide and as deep as the 30 foot setback requirements allow. The garage costs $15 per square foot. The total cost of the dwelling will be increased by what percent?

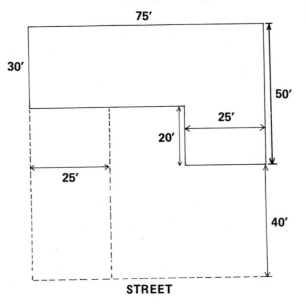

Solution

We must first find the cost of the original dwelling and the cost of the garage and compare these two numbers. The area of the original dwelling is found by dividing the diagram of the house into rectangles and summing the areas of the rectangles.

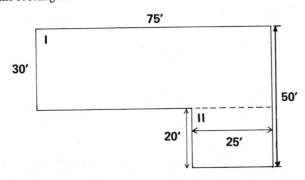

$$\text{Area I} = \text{Length} \times \text{Width} = 75 \text{ ft.} \times 30 \text{ ft.} = 2250 \text{ square ft.}$$
$$\text{Area II} = \text{Length} \times \text{Width} = 20 \text{ ft.} \times 25 \text{ ft.} = 500 \text{ square ft.}$$

Area I + II = 2250 sq. ft. + 500 sq. ft. = 2750 square ft.

If the area of the house is 2750 square feet and the cost is $30 per square foot, the house costs

$$2750 \times \$30 = \$82{,}500.$$

The garage is 25 feet wide. If it must be set back 30 feet from the street, it can only be 30 feet deep; i.e., 10 feet out from the part of the home which extends the most and 20 feet into the part of the house which extends the least, as shown below.

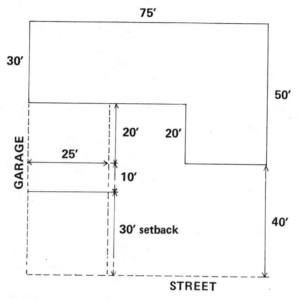

The area of the garage is 25 ft. × 30 ft. = 750 square ft. The cost of the garage is $15 × 750 = $11,250.

The cost of the house will be increased by $11,250 as compared to the original $82,500 (we always compare to the original cost).

$$\frac{\$11{,}250}{\$82{,}500} = .14 = 14\%$$

The cost of the dwelling will be increased by 14%.

Finally, percents show up in tax assessment problems, as follows:

3. A property is assessed for $20,000. Taxes are $2 per $100 of assessed valuation. If the assessed value is increased by $2000 and the tax rate increases by 25¢ per $100, find the percent increase in taxes.

Solution

First we find the original tax:

The assessed value is $20,000. The rate is $2 per $100. In $20,000 there are 200 one hundred dollar groups, each taxed $2.

$$\text{Original Tax} = 200 \times \$2 = \$400$$

Having found this, we can now find the new tax:

The assessed value is $20,000 + $2000 = $22,000. The tax rate is $2.25 per $100. In $22,000 there are 220 one hundred dollar groups, each taxed $2.25

$$New\ Tax = 220 \times \$2.25 = \$495$$

The increase in taxes is $495 - $400 = $95. Comparing the increase to the original tax we have the following:

$$\frac{\$95}{\$400} = .24 = 24\%$$

The tax increased by 24%.

12

CALCULATORS

The use of calculators during the Real Estate Licensing Exams is now permitted in many states. The calculator can perform many of the tedious computations previously performed manually and leaves more time for concentrating on problem-solving techniques. Like any other mechanical device, the calculator must be used with care. The following is a list of "do's" and "don'ts" associated with the use of a calculator:

1. Purchase a calculator to fit your needs. While there are many types of calculators ranging from very simple to quite complex, the calculator needed for the Real Estate Exams need have only four basic operations—addition, subtraction, multiplication, and division. Other functions such as percent and memory may be useful at times, but in turn may only become an additional concern. Purchase the simplest, easiest to operate calculator.

2. Practice with your calculator as much before the test as possible. Do not stop by your friend's house on the way to the exam to borrow his calculator and then expect to use it efficiently. Although most calculators are similar, it would be a shame to spend fifteen minutes of exam time trying to figure out how to turn on your calculator.

3. Some calculators go "crazy" before their battery runs out. The calculator doesn't have the courtesy to just shut down—it has the nerve to give incorrect answers. To make certain that your calculator is working correctly at all times, do a simple computation, such as 2×5 or $1 + 1$, right before working each problem. If you wait until you are halfway through the math problems to check your calculator, and then find it is malfunctioning, you will not be able to trust the answers you have already computed.

4. Write down each step of a problem as you are working on it. If your finger slips on the third step of a problem, you will have to begin all over again, unless you have written down the results of the first two steps.

While the calculator is a great helper, its only advantage is as a time saver. It is no substitute for your thoughtful consideration of the nature of the problem, organized planning for the solution of the problem, and careful monitoring of the calculator's computations.

13

SALESPERSON'S PRACTICE MATH EXAM

Directions: Read the following problems and select the correct answer.
Indicate your choice by writing in the blank space provided.

1. A broker earns 5 percent commission on the first $15,000 of a sale and $3\frac{1}{2}$ percent commission on anything above $15,000. If the broker earned a total of $1000 on a sale, what was the sales price?
   (A) $19,000
   (B) $22,142.86
   (C) $35,000
   (D) $7142.86

2. Mr. Krumholz netted $4000 on the sale of his property which he originally purchased for $25,000. He spent a total of $8000 for improvements. If the broker received 6 percent commission on the sale, what was the selling price?
   (A) $42,400
   (B) $35,000
   (C) $39,361.70
   (D) $30,851

3.

	AMOUNT OF LOAN	TERMS OF LOAN	MONTHLY PAYMENTS
$30,000–$40,000 homes	80%	$8\frac{3}{4}$% 25 years	$8/$1000

Using the table shown, what is the difference in monthly payments between a $30,000 home and a $40,000 home?
   (A) $64
   (B) $300
   (C) $80
   (D) $120

4. A home is currently appraised for $36,000 after having appreciated on the average of 2 percent a year for 5 years. What is the original purchase price?
   (A) $36,720
   (B) $38,975.38
   (C) $32,400
   (D) $32,727.27

5. A broker, salesperson, and listing salesperson share commission in the ratio of 4:3:2. On a $50,000 sale, with commission being earned at 7 percent, how much more than the listing salesperson does the broker earn?
    (A) $175
    (B) $1555.56
    (C) $1166.66
    (D) $777.78

6. An apartment house owner has the option to rent his 12 apartments for (1) $150 per month with utilities, or (2) $125 per month without utilities. If utilities cost $2000 per year for all apartments, with which option will the owner net more, and by how much?
    (A) $1600 more with Option 1
    (B) $3600 more with Option 1
    (C) $1600 more with Option 2
    (D) $5600 more with Option 1

7. What fraction best describes the area of the smaller rectangle compared to the area of the larger rectangle in the following diagram?

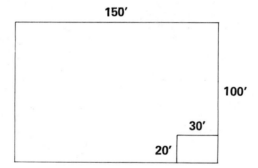

    (A) $\frac{6}{100}$
    (B) $\frac{25}{1}$
    (C) $\frac{1}{25}$
    (D) $\frac{1}{8}$

8. A $60,000 home is assessed for 55 percent of its value. If the tax rate is $.35/$10, what will be the tax bill?
    (A) $3255
    (B) $2100
    (C) $1300
    (D) $1155

9. Mr. Stevens sold his home on August 21 of this year. He pre-paid taxes of $3060 on January 1 for the fiscal year January 1 to December 31. What was the prorated tax the buyer owed Mr. Stevens?
    (A) $1104.15
    (B) $2210.85
    (C) $1955.85
    (D) $849.15

10. Mr. Bongaarts borrowed $20,000 for a business investment at an annual interest rate of 8 percent. If he kept the money for only 6 months and paid back the loan and interest in one lump sum, how much did he pay the bank after 6 months?
   (A) $1600
   (B) $20,800
   (C) $21,600
   (D) $800

11. A $30,000 home appreciated 10 percent each year over the previous year's value. What is it worth at the beginning of the third year?
   (A) $36,300
   (B) $39,000
   (C) $36,000
   (D) $39,930

12. Find the area of the shaded portion in the figure below.

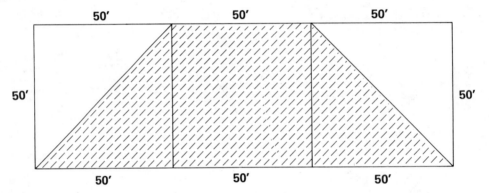

   (A) 7500 sq. ft.
   (B) 5000 sq. ft.
   (C) 2500 sq. ft.
   (D) 3750 sq. ft.

13. Find the average yearly rate of depreciation of a property if the original value is $20,000 and 5 years later it is worth $16,000.
   (A) 10%
   (B) 20%
   (C) 5%
   (D) 4%

14. Mr. Plawner pays $25 interest monthly on a loan which was taken at a 6 percent yearly interest rate. What was the amount of the loan?
   (A) $2000
   (B) $5000
   (C) $416.00
   (D) $1800

15. A listing salesperson earns $12\frac{1}{2}$ percent of the total 6 percent commission on the sale of all homes he has listed. How much commission does he earn on the sale of a $42,000 home?
   (A) $5250
   (B) $777
   (C) $3150
   (D) $315

16.   A salesperson earns a salary of $500 per month. In addition he earns 7 percent commission on all sales.
      What were his annual sales if his total yearly income was $18,000?
      (A) $257,142.85
      (B) $240,000
      (C) $171,428.57
      (D) $35,000

17.   What would be the difference in taxes on a $15,000 assessment of property if the tax rate was $.04 per
      dollar as compared to $.05 per dollar?
      (A) $200
      (B) $150
      (C) $1250
      (D) $1500

18.   If insurance for a married couple costs $240 per year and $132 for just the husband or just the wife, what
      is the difference per month if both are insured separately rather than as a married couple?
      (A) $2
      (B) $9
      (C) $4.50
      (D) $1

19.   A man pays $45 per month to principal and interest. The mortgage is $5000. What is the principal owed
      after the first monthly payment has been applied if the annual interest rate is 7 percent per annum?
      (A) $4984.17
      (B) $4650
      (C) $15.83
      (D) $4010

20.   Mrs. Weisberg sold her antiques, which were originally purchased for $1200, for $1500. What is the rate of
      profit?
      (A) 120%
      (B) 25%
      (C) 125%
      (D) 20%

ANSWER KEY

1. B	6. A	11. A	16. C
2. C	7. C	12. B	17. B
3. A	8. D	13. D	18. A
4. D	9. A	14. B	19. A
5. D	10. B	15. D	20. B

Solutions to Salesperson's Practice Math Exam

1.   **(B)** The Commission earned was 5 percent on the first $15,000 or 5% × $15,000 = .05 × $15,000 = $750.
     Since a total of $1000 was earned, we know that the sales price was at least $15,000. We are now looking
     for the remaining part of the sales price which earned $1000 – $750 = $250 commission, earned at a rate

of $3\frac{1}{2}$ percent. Using the triangle method to find the remaining part of the sales price

Selling Price = ?
Rate of Commission = $3\frac{1}{2}\% = .035$
Commission = \$250

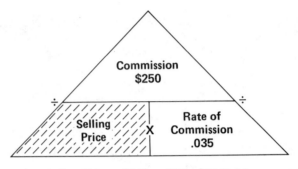

Selling Price = \$250 ÷ .035 = \$7142.86

Adding \$15,000 to \$7142.86, the Total Sales Price = \$22,142.86.

2. **(C)** Using the circle diagram

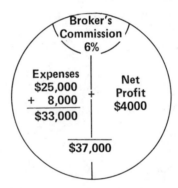

94% of Selling Price = \$37,000
or
.94 × Selling Price = \$37,000

Putting this into the triangle

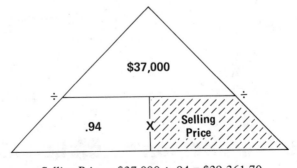

Selling Price = \$37,000 ÷ .94 = \$39,361.70

The Selling Price is \$39,361.70.

3. **(A)** $30,000 home

$$\text{Loan} = 80\% \text{ of } \$30,000 = .80 \times \$30,000 = \$24,000$$
$$\text{Monthly payment} = \$8 \text{ per } \$1000$$
$$\text{Monthly payment} = \$8 \times 24 = \$192$$

$40,000 home

$$\text{Loan} = 80\% \text{ of } \$40,000 = .80 \times \$40,000 = \$32,000$$
$$\text{Monthly payment} = \$8 \times 32 = \$256$$

Difference in montly payments is $256 - $192 = $64.

4. **(D)**

$$A\% = 5 \times 2\% = 10\% \ .$$
$$(100 + A)\% = (100 + 10)\% = 110\% = 1.10$$
$$\text{Present Price} = \$36,000$$
$$\text{Original Price} = ?$$

Using the triangle

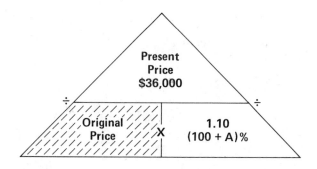

$$\text{Original Price} = \$36,000 \div 1.10 = \$32,727.27$$

The Original Price is $32,727.27.

5. **(D)**

$$\text{Total Commission} = ?$$
$$\text{Selling Price} = \$50,000$$
$$\text{Rate of Commission} = 7\% = .07$$

Using the triangle

Commission $50,000 × .07 = $3500

Broker gets 4 parts, salesperson gets 3 parts and listing salesperson gets 2 parts = 9 parts total

$$\$3500 \div 9 = \$388.89 \text{ per part}$$

Broker gets 4 × $388.89 = $1555.56
Salesperson gets 3 × $388.89 = $1166.67
Listing Salesperson gets 2 × $388.89 = $777.78
The broker earns $1555.56 – $777.78 or $777.78 more than the listing salesperson.

6. **(A)**
Option 1

Gross Income = $150 × 12(apts.) × 12(months) = $21,600
Net Profit = $21,600 – $2000 = $19,600

Option 2

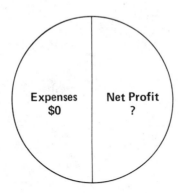

Gross Income = $125 × 12(apts.) × 12(months) = $18,000
Net Profit = $18,000 – 0 = $18,000
The owner would net $19,600 – $18,000 or $1600 more with Option 1.

7. **(C)**

Area large rectangle = 150 ft. × 100 ft. = 15,000 square ft.
Area small rectangle = 30 ft. × 20 ft. = 600 square ft.

To compare the small rectangle to the large rectangle we write:

$$\frac{600 \text{ sq. ft.}}{15,000 \text{ sq. ft.}} = \frac{1}{25}$$

The area of the small rectangle in relation to the large rectangle is $\frac{1}{25}$.

8. **(D)**

$$\text{Actual Value} = \$60,000$$
$$\text{Assessed Value} = 55\% \text{ of } \$60,000 = .55 \times \$60,000 = \$33,000$$
$$\text{Tax Rate} = \$.35/\$10$$

There are $\$33,000 \div \$10$ or 3300 groups of ten dollars in $\$33,000$.
Tax Bill $= 3300 \times \$.35 = \$1155$.
The tax bill will be $\$1155$.

9. **(A)** $\$3060$ taxes for the year would mean $\$3060 \div 12 = \$255$ per month.

Mr. Stevens lived in the house for the following months of the fiscal year:

$$\text{January through July} = 7 \text{ months}$$
$$20 \text{ days in August} = \tfrac{2}{3} \text{ month} = .67 \text{ month}$$

Mr. Stevens lived in the house for 7.67 months.

The buyer lived in the house for the following months of the fiscal year:

$$10 \text{ days in August} = \tfrac{1}{3} \text{ month} = .33 \text{ month}$$
$$\text{September through December} = 4 \text{ months}$$

The buyer lived in the house for 4.33 months.
(Note: 7.67 months + 4.33 months = 12 months = 1 year.)
The buyer owed Mr. Stevens $4.33 \times \$255 = \$1104.15$.

10. **(B)**

$$P \times R = I$$
$$P = \$20,000$$
$$R = 8\% = .08$$
$$I(\text{yearly}) = ?$$

Placing this information into the triangle

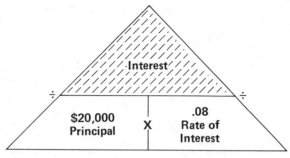

$$\text{Yearly Interest} = \$20,000 \times .08 = \$1600$$
$$6 \text{ Month's Interest} = \$1600 \div 2 = \$800$$

Mr. Bongaarts, at the end of 6 months, paid the bank a total of $\$20,000 + \$800 = \$20,800$.

11. **(A)**

$$\text{Original Price (beginning 1st year)} = \$30,000$$
$$(100 + A)\% = 110\% = 1.10$$
$$\text{Present Price (end 1st year)} = ?$$

Placing this information into the triangle

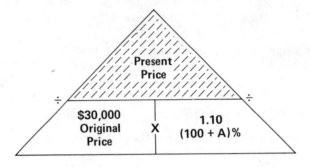

Present Price (end 1st year) = $30,000 × 1.10 = $33,000.

Starting again:

Original Price (beginning 2nd year) = $33,000
(100 + A)% = 110% = 1.10
Present Price (end 2nd year) = ?

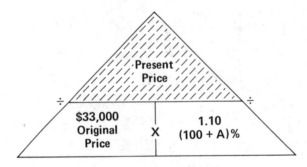

Present Price (end 2nd year) = $33,000 × 1.10 = $36,300.
Value at the end of the 2nd year is the same as the beginning of the 3rd year.

At the beginning of the 3rd year the property is worth $36,300.

12. **(B)**
<u>Method 1</u>

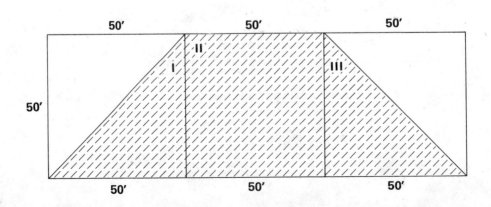

$$\text{Area figure I} = \frac{\text{Leg} \times \text{Leg}}{2}$$

$$= \frac{50 \text{ ft.} \times 50 \text{ ft.}}{2}$$

$$= \frac{2500 \text{ sq. ft.}}{2}$$

$$= 1250 \text{ square ft.}$$

$$\text{Area figure II} = \text{Length} \times \text{Width}$$
$$= 50 \text{ ft.} \times 50 \text{ ft.}$$
$$= 2500 \text{ square ft.}$$

$$\text{Area figure III} = \frac{\text{Leg} \times \text{Leg}}{2}$$

$$= \frac{50 \text{ ft.} \times 50 \text{ ft.}}{2}$$

$$= \frac{2500 \text{ sq. ft.}}{2}$$

$$= 1250 \text{ square ft.}$$

Areas I + II + III = 1250 sq. ft. + 2500 sq. ft. + 1250 sq. ft. = 5000 square ft.

Method 2

(using the fact that the shaded portion is a trapezoid)

$$\text{Area} = \frac{(\text{Base} + \text{Base}) \times \text{Height}}{2}$$

$$= \frac{(50 \text{ ft.} + 150 \text{ ft.}) \times 50 \text{ ft.}}{2}$$

$$= \frac{200 \times 50}{2}$$

$$= 5000 \text{ square ft.}$$

13. **(D)**

$$\text{Original Price} = \$20,000$$
$$\text{Present Price} = \$16,000$$
$$(100 - D)\% = ?$$

Placing this information into the triangle

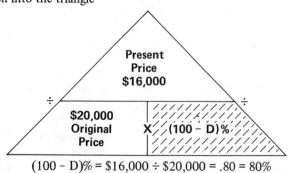

$(100 - D)\% = \$16,000 \div \$20,000 = .80 = 80\%$

If $(100 - D)\% = 80\%$, then $D\% = 20\%$.
$20\% \div 5 = 4\%$ per year (on the average).

14. **(B)**

$$P \times R = I$$
$$P = ?$$
$$R = 6\%$$
$$I = \$25 \times 12 = \$300$$

Placing this information into the triangle

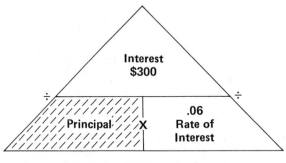

Principal = $\$300 \div .06 = \$5000$

The amount of the loan is \$5,000.

15. **(D)** First we find the total commission.

$$\text{Commission} = ?$$
$$\text{Selling Price} = \$42,000$$
$$\text{Rate of Commission} = 6\% = .06$$

Placing this information into the triangle

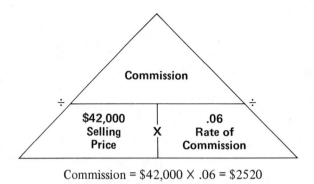

Commission = $\$42,000 \times .06 = \$2520$

$12\frac{1}{2}\%$ of $\$2520 = .125 \times \$2520 = \$315$ for the listing salesperson.

16. **(C)** A salary of \$500 per month = $\$500 \times 12$ or \$6000 per year. A total of \$18,000 was earned for the year. Therefore, \$18,000 - \$6000 or \$12,000 was earned through commission on sales at the rate of 7 percent. To find the amount of sales we use the triangle.

$$\text{Commission} = \$12,000$$
$$\text{Rate of Commission} = 7\% = .07$$
$$\text{Selling Price} = ?$$

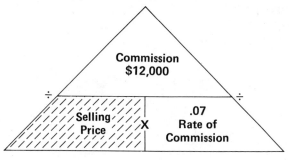

Selling Price = $12,000 ÷ .07 = $171,428.57

His annual sales were $171,428.57.

17.   **(B)** In $15,000 there are 15,000 units of one dollar.

$$\$.04 \times \$15,000 = \$600$$
$$\$.05 \times \$15,000 = \$750$$

The difference in taxes is $750 - $600 = $150.

18.   **(A)** Insurance for a married couple is $240 per year or $240 ÷ 12 = $20 per month.

Insurance for just the husband or just the wife is $132 per year or $132 ÷ 12 = $11 per month. Insurance for both the husband and the wife when insured separately would be $11 × 2 = $22 per month.

The difference if they were insured separately would be $22 - $20 = $2 per month.

19.   **(A)**

This circle represents the $45 monthly payment.

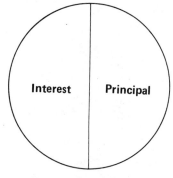

Interest (yearly) = ?
Principal = $5000
Rate of Interest = 7% = .07

Placing this information into the triangle

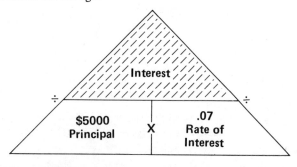

Interest (yearly) = $5000 × .07 = $350.
Monthly interest is $350 ÷ 12 = $29.17.
Now we have

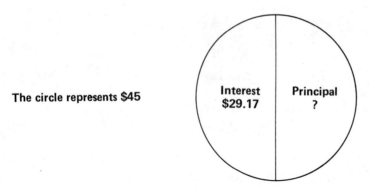

The circle represents $45

$45 - $29.17 or $15.83 goes to reducing principal.

After the first monthly payment $5000 - $15.83 = $4984.17 is left of the mortgage.

20. **(B)**

Original Investment = $1200
Profit = $1500 - $1200 = $300
Rate of Profit = ?

Placing this information into the triangle

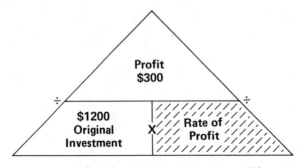

Rate of Profit = $300 ÷ 1200 = .25 = 25%

The Rate of Profit is 25 percent.

14

BROKER'S PRACTICE MATH EXAM

Directions: Read the following problems and select the correct answer.

Indicate your choice by writing in the blank space provided.

1. In the following diagram, 3 acres will be left for parking facilities. What percent will be for parking?

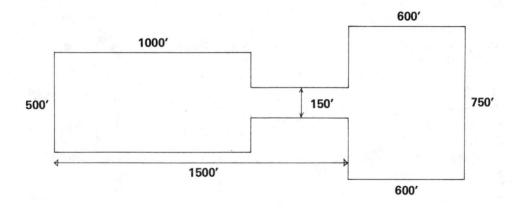

(A) $12\frac{1}{2}\%$
(B) 8%
(C) 11%
(D) 16%

2. A property is assessed at $18,000. Taxes are $3.50 per $100 of assessed value. If the assessed value increased by $4000 and the tax rate is raised by $.40 per $100, by what percent will the taxes be increased?
(A) 27%
(B) 13%
(C) 36%
(D) 73%

3. A home has been appreciating in value on the average of 2 percent per year for 10 years. If its current value is $58,000, what was the original value?
(A) $56,862.75
(B) $46,400
(C) $69,600
(D) $48,333.33

4. Mr. Sandler wants a net return of 12 percent on his investment which has a rental income of $20,000 and expenses of $400 per month. What is the most he can offer to pay for the property?
   (A) $126,666.67
   (B) $2976
   (C) $163,333.33
   (D) $206,666.67

5. The seller of a home wants to net $15,000 on the sale of his property. His mortgage balance is $18,000 and his equity is $15,000. What must the selling price be if he must pay 7 percent commission to a broker?
   (A) $19,354.84
   (B) $51,360
   (C) $51,613
   (D) $44,640

6. A home is built on a 100 ft. by 150 ft. lot. It occupies 20 percent of the lot. If the home costs $36,000, find the cost of the home per square foot.
   (A) $2.40
   (B) $24
   (C) $30
   (D) $12

7. A landlord leases office space of 125,000 square feet for $8 per square foot. His total expenses per year are $90,000. An investor wants to buy the property and net 10 percent on the investment. What is the maximum price he should offer the landlord for the property?
   (A) $91,000,000
   (B) $10,900,000
   (C) $50,000
   (D) $9,100,000

8. A property worth $40,000 depreciates 10 percent each year. What is the property worth after 2 years?
   (A) $38,000
   (B) $32,400
   (C) $48,000
   (D) $32,000

9. A house is 2500 square feet. It was originally purchased for $50,000. If it's currently worth $60,000, what is the increase in worth per square foot?
   (A) $24
   (B) $.25
   (C) $16
   (D) $4

10. Mr. Smith bought 100 acres at $1000 per acre. Taxes are $1000 a year. After 8 years he sold the property and earned 12 percent gross profit. What was the sales price?
    (A) $103,040
    (B) $95,040
    (C) $91,800
    (D) $120,960

11. A lot is purchased for $1500. Annual maintenance expenses are $250. What must the selling price be after a year if a gross profit of 11 percent on the investment is desired?
    (A) $1387.50

(B) $2500
(C) $1557.50
(D) $1942.50

12. In the following diagram, what percent of the lot does the building shown occupy?

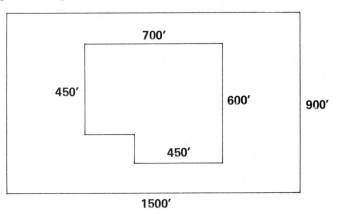

(A) 43%
(B) 35.2%
(C) 28%
(D) 65%

13. A property capitalized at 12 percent has a net value of $250,000. If the net income is 90 percent of the gross income, find the gross income.
(A) $57,000
(B) $27,000
(C) $33,333.33
(D) $32,000

14. Ten years ago a property was worth $75,000. It is currently worth only $60,000. Find the average annual rate of depreciation.
(A) 2%
(B) 25%
(C) 8%
(D) $2\frac{1}{2}$%

15. A broker and a salesperson share commission in the ratio of 5:3. On a $60,000 sale at a 6 percent commission rate, find each one's share of the commission.
(A) broker gets $2250, salesperson gets $1350
(B) broker gets $1350, salesperson gets $2250
(C) broker gets $720, salesperson gets $1200
(D) broker gets $2000, salesperson gets $1600

ANSWER KEY

1. A	6. D	11. D
2. C	7. D	12. C
3. D	8. B	13. C
4. A	9. D	14. A
5. C	10. D	15. A

Solutions to Broker's Practice Math Exam

1. **(A)**

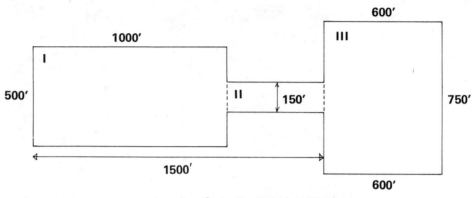

Area figure I = Length × Width
= 1000 ft. × 500 ft.
= 500,000 square ft.

Area figure II = Length × Width
= 500 ft. × 150 ft.
= 75,000 square ft.

Area figure III = Length × Width
= 750 ft. × 600 ft.
= 450,000 square ft.

Area I + II + III = 500,000 sq. ft. + 75,000 sq. ft. + 450,000 sq. ft.
= 1,025,000 square ft.

Since 43,560 square feet = 1 acre, to find how many acres there are in 1,025,000 square feet we divide by 43,560.

$$1,025,000 \div 43,560 = 24$$

There is a total of 24 acres.
If 3 acres are for parking, then $\frac{3}{24}$ or $\frac{1}{8}$ is reserved for parking.

To change $\frac{1}{8}$ to a percent: $1 \div 8 = .125 = 12.5\% = 12\frac{1}{2}\%$.
$12\frac{1}{2}$ percent will be reserved for parking.

2. **(C)**

$18,000 ÷ $100 = 180 groups of one hundred dollars.
180 × $3.50 = $630

The original tax is $630.

$18,000 + $4000 = $22,000 (new assessed value)
$22,000 ÷ $100 = 220 groups of one hundred dollars
Tax rate = $3.50 + .40 = $3.90 per $100
220 × $3.90 = $858

The new tax is $858.

The tax increased by $858 - $630 = $228.
Comparing the increase to the original tax we have:

$$\frac{\$228}{\$630} = .36 = 36\%$$

The tax increased by 36%.

3. **(D)**

$$A = 10 \times 2\% = 20\%$$
$$(100 + A)\% = (100 + 20)\% = 120\% = 1.20$$
$$\text{Present Price} = \$58,000$$
$$\text{Original Price} = ?$$

Placing this information into the triangle

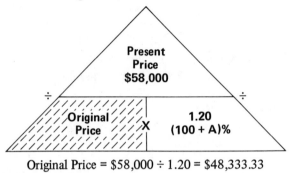

Original Price = $58,000 ÷ 1.20 = $48,333.33

The original value was $48,333.33.

4. **(A)**

$$\text{Value} \times \text{Rate of Capitalization} = \text{Net Profit}$$
$$\text{Rate of Capitalization} = 12\% = .12$$
$$\text{Net Profit} = \text{Gross Income} - \text{Expenses}$$
$$\text{Gross Income} = \$20,000$$
$$\text{Expenses} = \$400 \times 12 = \$4800$$
$$\text{Net Profit} = \$20,000 - 4800 = \$15,200$$
$$\text{Value} = ?$$

Placing this information into the triangle

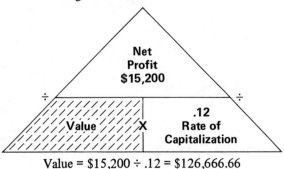

Value = $15,200 ÷ .12 = $126,666.66

He can offer $126,666.66 for the property.

5. **(C)** Using the circle diagram, if the equity is $15,000 and the mortgage balance is $18,000, then the investor must have bought the property for $15,000 + $18,000 or $33,000.

Expenses = $33,000
Net Profit = $15,000

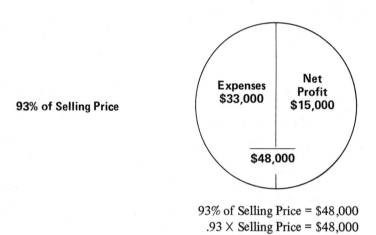

93% of Selling Price

93% of Selling Price = $48,000
.93 × Selling Price = $48,000

Placing this information into the triangle

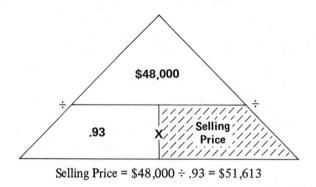

Selling Price = $48,000 ÷ .93 = $51,613

The Selling Price must be $51,613.

6. **(D)**

Area lot = Length × Width
= 100 ft. × 150 ft.
= 15,000 square ft.

The house occupies 20 percent of the lot or 20% × 15,000 sq. ft. or .20 × 15,000 sq. ft. = 3000 square ft.

The cost of the home is $36,000. Cost per square foot is $36,000 ÷ 3000 sq. ft. = $12 per square foot.

7. **(D)**

Value × Rate of Capitalization = Net Profit
Value = ?

Rate of Capitalization = 10% = .10
Net Profit = Gross Income – Expenses
Gross Income = $125,000 × 8 = $1,000,000
Expenses = $90,000
Net Profit = $1,000,000 – $90,000 = $910,000

Placing this information into the triangle

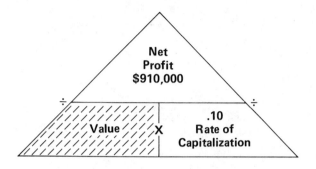

Value = $910,000 ÷ .10 = $9,100,000

He should offer a maximum of $9,100,000.

8. **(B)**

Original Price (beginning 1st year) = $40,000
(100 – D)% = (100 – 10)% = 90% = .90
Present Price (end 1st year) = ?

Placing this information into the triangle

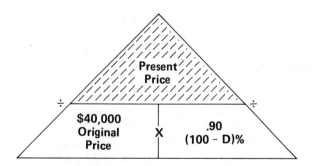

Present Price (end 1st year) = $40,000 × .90 = $36,000

Now starting once again:

Original Price (beginning 2nd year) = $36,000
(100 – D)% = (100 – 10)% = 90% = .90
Present Price (end 2nd year) = ?

Placing this information into the triangle

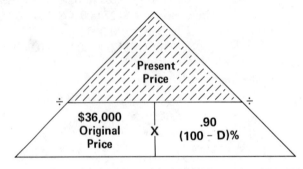

Present Price (end 2nd year) = $36,000 × .90 = $32,400

After two years the property is worth $32,400.

9.   **(D)** There is a difference in price of $60,000 - $50,000 = $10,000.

$10,000 ÷ 2500 sq. ft. = $4 per square foot increase

10.   **(D)**

Original Investment = Purchase Price + Expenses
Purchase Price = $1000 × 100 = $100,000
Expenses = $1000 × 8 = $8000
Original Investment = $100,000 + $8000 = $108,000
Rate of Profit = 12% = .12
Profit = ?

Placing this information into the triangle

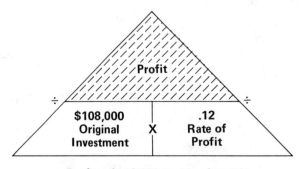

Profit = $108,000 × .12 = $12,960
Selling Price = Original Investment + Profit
= $108,000 + 12,960 = $120,960

The Selling Price is $120,960.

11.   **(D)**

Original Investment = Purchase Price + Expenses
= $1500 + $250 = $1750
Rate of Profit = 11% = .11
Profit = ?

Placing this information into the triangle

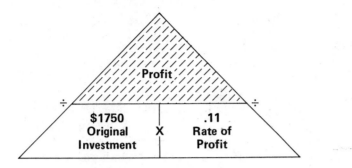

Profit = $1750 × .11 = $192.50
Selling Price = Original Investment + Profit
= $1750 + 192.50 = $1942.50

The Selling Price must be $1942.50.

12. (C) Area lot = 1500 ft. × 900 ft. = 1,350,000 square ft.

Area building:

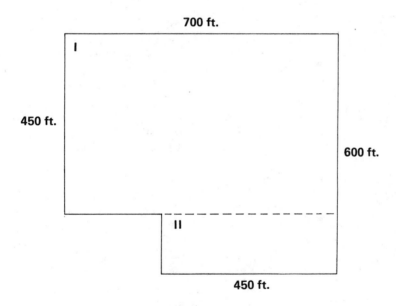

Area I = Length × Width
= 700 ft. × 450 ft.
= 315,000 square ft.

Area II = Length × Width
= 450 ft. × 150 ft.
= 67,500 square ft.

Area I + II = 315,000 sq. ft. + 67,500 sq. ft.
= 382,500 square ft.

Area of the building compared to the area of the lot is:

$$\frac{382,500}{1,350,000} = .28 = 28\%$$

The building is 28 percent of the lot.

13. **(C)**

Value × Rate of Capitalization = Net Profit
Value = $250,000
Rate of Capitalization = 12% = .12
Net Profit = ?

Placing this information into the triangle

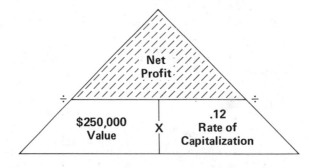

Net Profit = $250,000 × .12 = $30,000

The net profit is 90 percent of the gross income.

Therefore: 90% × Gross Income = $30,000.
                          .90 × Gross Income = $30,000

Placing this information into the triangle

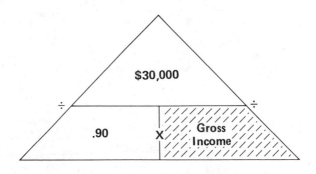

Gross Income = $30,000 ÷ .90 = $33,333.33

The Gross Income is $33,333.33.

14. **(A)**

Original Price = $75,000
Present Price = $60,000
(100 − D)% = ?

Placing this information into the triangle

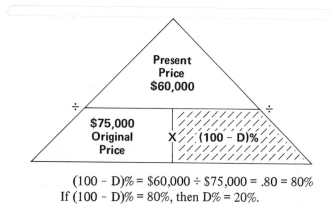

(100 − D)% = $60,000 ÷ $75,000 = .80 = 80%
If (100 − D)% = 80%, then D% = 20%.

The average rate of depreciation per year is 20% ÷ 10 = 2% per year.

15. **(A)**

Commission = ?
Selling Price = $60,000
Rate of Commission = 6% = .06

Placing this information into the triangle

Commission = $60,000 × .06 = $3600

5 parts for the broker and 3 parts for the salesperson = 8 parts.

$3600 ÷ 8 = $450 per part
Broker gets $450 × 5 = $2250
Salesperson gets $450 × 3 = $1350.